THE NEW 90 MINUTE RESUME

PEGGY SCHMIDT

Peterson's
Princeton, New Jersey

Visit Peterson's at http://www.petersons.com

Peterson's Career Focus Books: *helping people make successful job choices, maximize career potential, and stay competitive in today's workplace*

Library of Congress Cataloging-in-Publication Data
Schmidt, Peggy J.
    The new 90-minute resume / Peggy Schmidt.
        p.   cm.
    Rev. ed. of: The 90-minute resume. 2nd ed.
    ISBN 1-56079-633-2
    1. Résumés (Employment)   2. Applications for positions.
    I. Schmidt, Peggy J. 90-minute resume.   II. Title.
    HF5383.S325   1996
    650.14—dc20   96-22189
                                                                        CIP

Editorial direction by Carol Hupping   Composition by Gary Rozmierski
Production supervision by Bernadette Boylan   Creative direction by Linda Huber
Copyediting by Kathleen Salazar   Interior design by Cynthia Boone
Proofreading by Joanne Schauffele

Printed in the United States of America

10 9 8 7 6 5 4 3 2 1

CONTENTS

ACKNOWLEDGMENTS

My deepest thanks to those who have contributed their ideas to this and previous editions of *The 90-Minute Resume*.

Richard J. Chagnon, senior vice president, Career Management Services, Right Associates, Philadelphia, Pennsylvania

John D. Erdlen, president, Strategic Outsourcing, Inc., Wellesley, Massachusetts

Susan Gordon, president, The Lynne Palmer Agency, New York, New York

Joseph Hnilo, vice president, Resumix, Santa Clara, California

Gregory Morse, vice president, Restrac, Dedham, Massachusetts

Kim La Barber, manager, Marketing & Communication, Intellifax, San Jose, California

My editor, Carol Hupping, and the Peterson's staff

HOW THIS BOOK CAN HELP YOU

Every job hunter needs a resume. It's the document that employers who are hiring have come to expect. Resumes can be used for several purposes in a job hunt:

- To initiate contact with an employer

- To give to contacts who are in a position to recommend you to an employer (so they can send it on to that employer or talk specifically about your skills and experiences) To respond to help-wanted ads

- To use when applying to temporary or permanent employment agencies

- To input into an on-line job database

- To attach to a job application

- To give to an interviewer (who may not be able to locate your resume when you come in or who may not have received a copy of it from the person you first interviewed with at the company)

Still, most job hunters, understandably, do not look forward to writing or revising a resume. It's a daunting organizational task, and if you're not someone who regularly writes, selecting the right words can also be intimidating.

The good news: *The New 90-Minute Resume* can help make writing or revising your resume more manageable *and* more enjoyable. The idea behind this book is simple: If you ask someone to act as coach, to ask you questions about your experience and help you come up with clear, concise language to describe it (or if you're an experienced employee, help you critique the pluses and minuses of your current resume), you can create a strong selling piece that can help you land interviews. You may also want to buy the companion book, *The 90-Minute Interview Prep*, to help you get ready for and do your best in interviews.

The New 90-Minute Resume is designed to help all kinds of job hunters, including people who:

- Are looking for their first jobs

- Hope to move up in the same field (like a research associate who wants to become a senior researcher)

- Want to make a lateral move to a related skill area within their fields (for example, a graphic designer who wants to become a desktop-publishing specialist)

1

- Are hoping to change industries but remain in the same type of job (for example, an alcohol and drug abuse counselor who now works in an inpatient hospital program but who wants to work in the employee-assistance program of a corporation)

- Plan to change fields (for example, a stockbroker who wants to break into sports marketing; a flight attendant who hopes to become a cosmetics manufacturer's representative; a real estate broker who wants to become an interior designer)

- Want to return to work after taking time off (to raise children, care for a sick relative, recover from an accident or illness)

The first edition of *The 90-Minute Resume* came out in 1990. Since then, two revised editions have been published. *The New 90-Minute Resume* incorporates the latest developments in job hunting. The use of automated candidate-tracking systems and developments on-line (both on the Internet and subscriber on-line services) are changing the way employers identify potential candidates and the way employees look for jobs. You'll learn more about these developments in Chapter 11, Put Your Resume to Work. You will learn what you need to do to make sure your resume is read and easily interpreted by both a person and resume software. In that chapter, there is also a section devoted to how to identify employers using resources on-line.

Also new in this book are more sample resumes, so you'll have plenty to choose from to suit your needs. The computer disk that comes with this book allows you to print out as many copies of the suggested work sheets as you need. And it also contains resume samples that can help you create a great-looking resume fast.

Finally, a philosophical aside: Believe in yourself. Even if you think that you have done only ordinary things, you are a special person with unique experiences and skills. With the right skills and/or experience, you can get a better job than you now have or last had.

Start with the conviction that the resume you create is the first step in a new direction. The process of creating your resume will help you focus your job objective and organize your experiences if you follow the steps suggested in *The New 90-Minute Resume*. Knowing where you are going and how your past jobs have prepared you to take that next step is critical to convincing an employer that you are the right candidate. Expressing your ambition and accomplishments on paper will give you confidence and direction as you begin your job search.

While I cannot provide individual resume services, I would like to hear from you if you would like to share your experiences using the 90-minute resume process. You can e-mail me at PeggyNCC@aol.com or write me in care of Peterson's, 202 Carnegie Center, P.O. Box 2123, Princeton, New Jersey, 08543-2123.

Peggy Schmidt
August, 1996

1 ▶ HOW THE 90-MINUTE RESUME PROCESS WORKS

You can write or revise your resume in a relatively short period of time by using the method I have developed from years of teaching resume-writing workshops and working with individuals to perfect their resumes. It's called the coach approach.

Few tasks are more daunting than trying to summarize your work life on paper and present it in a way that says, "I'm a terrific candidate. Call me." Figuring out what to include or emphasize and what to leave out or discard is difficult. But if you enlist the help of another person who has had the experience of writing his or her own resume or even evaluating others', your progress will be quicker and the results stronger. Your coach can provide an objective sounding board and perspective that will make those decisions easier. If you have a resume that needs updating, a coach can give you ideas on how it can be changed and improved. If you're creating a resume from scratch, he or she can ask questions that will help the two of you get the most important information down on paper.

If you were to write or revise your resume on your own, chances are good you would spend hours, maybe days, tinkering with it. The beauty of the 90-minute process is that by following clearly defined steps and using another person—your coach—as a sounding board, an interviewer, and a resource, you can produce an even better product in a much shorter time. This book contains all the information the two of you need to produce a resume that will portray you at your best.

Think of your resume as you would a coming attraction for a movie; if the preview is enticing, you are going to want to see the film when it is released. Similarly, a carefully conceived resume can result in a call for an interview.

What makes for a winning resume? First, it must be visually inviting, that is clean and highly readable and scannable—type that is dark and clean and contains no italics or underlines. Second, it should highlight what you have to offer to a particular employer—your skills, knowledge, academic credentials, and experience—in an easy-to-follow format. Third, and perhaps most important, it should highlight the results of your efforts—your accomplishments—in specific language.

Before you schedule a session with your coach, skim through the book to get an idea of how it works. If your coach has time, a quick read of the book is the best way for him or her to prepare. If that's not possible, have your coach read the entire first two chapters and the Coach Guidelines that are interspersed throughout the book.

An hour and a half is a realistic time period in which to produce a final working draft (producing the final product is discussed in Chapter 10, Design Your Resume, and is not included in the 90 minutes). Before you get together with your coach, you will need to do some preparation that will allow you to proceed smoothly. This includes putting together your Fact Sheets (Chapter 2) and developing a job target (Chapter 3).

The 90-minute process itself consists of six major parts:

1. Reviewing your job target

2. Critiquing your current resume (resume revisers)

3. Using the interview method to create or expand information

4. Translating your notes into resume language

5. Creating a working draft

6. Perfecting your content

(In addition, Chapter 4 contains an extra 35-minute exercise—For Career Changers Only: The Matching Game—which is not counted in the 90 minutes.) The times allotted for each step are a general guideline; you may find that you do not need as much or that you need more. The important thing is to take the time you feel you need to successfully complete the step, even if you exceed the suggested time.

If you are not changing careers, move ahead to Selecting the Right Coach (page 6). If you are changing careers, read the following section.

ADVANCE WORK FOR CAREER CHANGERS ONLY

Changing careers is not something that can be done lightly or easily, which is why you have more advance work to do before revising your resume than job hunters who are hoping to move up in the same field, change industries, or make a lateral move within an industry.

You will also follow several different steps in creating your new resume. "When you are changing direction, it's critical for your resume to communicate what about your background makes your experience a good fit for a new type of job," says Susan Gordon, president of the Lynne Palmer Agency, a personnel agency in New York City that specializes in placing candidates in book and magazine publishing. "If you have analyzed your situation clearly, a potential employer is more likely to see things your way," she adds.

To do that in a systematic way, you and your coach will be given instructions on how to find parallels between your past experience and your new job target and how to translate those similarities into convincing resume language.

Deciding to look for a job in a new field requires a lot of soul searching and researching—soul searching because you may have to forgo status and perks (not to mention income) when you make the leap to a new career; researching because you cannot make a well-informed judgment about what you are going to do next without it.

It's critical to develop a resume that reflects your carefully thought-through decision, and this book will help you do just that. Your current resume is a summary of what you have already done, not what you hope to do, which is why it's important to do the following before overhauling your resume:

- Conduct an analysis of your skills, interests, and talent to determine your ideal job

- Read everything you can about the field and type of job(s) you have pinpointed

- Talk to a variety of people who work in the field about their experiences

- Identify the hurdles you face breaking into a new field

- Weigh the pros and cons of making such a change

- Complete educational or licensing requirements (or be close to completing them)

Another fact worth keeping in mind: Unless there is a shortage of highly qualified people to fill the kind of job you hope to get, the more difficult it will be to convince an employer to hire you over someone who has been working steadily in the field and accumulating experiences that build on each other.

When the number of exceptional candidates is low, on the other hand, an employer is more willing to risk hiring someone whose experience varies widely from what's expected. Says John D. Erdlen, president of Strategic Outsourcing, Inc., "What can make all the difference in the world is a guardian angel—a mentor type—who is willing to vouch for you and say, 'She's worth the risk.'"

The risk, as many employers see it, is that the career changer may take longer to get up to speed or is less tuned into the nuances of the job than the person who has followed a more traditional job path. An even bigger fear is that the career changer will not be able to perform as well in the job. That's why having someone such as an ex-boss who knows your work habits and capabilities and can provide reassurance to a potential employer is a big plus.

In the absence of a guardian angel (or sometimes before a guardian angel can step in), you have to make your own case that you should seriously be considered as a candidate. If your first introduction to an employer is your resume, it's essential that it communicates that:

1. You have done your research and understand what the position requires

2. You are serious about making the change

3. You would be a great candidate for the job

Your coach can play an important support role in helping you accomplish that. Ideally, your coach should be someone who currently works in or who has had experience in the field you hope to switch to. The advantage of such a coach is that he or she knows the jargon, has a handle on the thinking of people in that profession, and can make suggestions you can rely on. If you cannot enlist the help of such a person, don't worry; an intelligent and thoughtful person who has the characteristics of the coach discussed in the next section will be fine.

SELECTING THE RIGHT COACH

Now that you have an overview of where you are going, you can start your first assignment: identifying the right person to help you.

The ideal coach is someone who is familiar with your field and who has at least as much, if not more, experience than do you. Beyond that, the coach should be a good conversationalist and have reasonably good writing skills. After all, his or her job is to ask you questions and get you to talk about yourself. Beyond that, your coach needs to be able to help you select the right words to convey your strengths on paper.

Your coach may be a colleague (who can be trusted to keep a confidence), an ex-colleague, someone you know through a professional organization, or a former client or classmate. If there is no one who readily fits the bill, a good bet is any experienced professional whose judgment you respect. That person might be a relative, neighbor, or someone you know through community or church activities.

Your spouse (or the person with whom you are romantically involved) may be the most convenient person to recruit as coach, but keep this in mind: He or she will probably not be as objective in his or her critique or suggestions as someone less emotionally involved in your life.

The most important thing is that your coach take the responsibility seriously and be willing to spend 90 minutes to give you thoughtful feedback and ask good questions. The following section will help your coach understand his or her role in the 90-minute process. You can print out this section by using the disk that comes with this book.

A CRASH COURSE FOR COACHES

You are about to play an enjoyable and important role as coach in this unique resume creation process. Just what are you expected to do? Three things:

1. Critique the job hunter's current resume (unless the job hunter is writing a resume for the first time). Your perspective will be invaluable because you can help spot information gaps, unclear language, and organizational problems, among other things.

2. Interview the job hunter. Your questions to the job hunter (a list will be provided) make the job of getting information down on paper an easy one.

3. Provide feedback and ideas. As you work with the job hunter on choosing words to communicate his or her background and organizing the information in a way that it can be easily followed, you can act as a sounding board and suggest ways of doing things that may not have otherwise occurred to a person working alone.

You will find the role of coach easier if you have had experience evaluating resumes (as an employer) or if you have experience in the field in which the job hunter hopes to find his or her next job. If you have neither, rest assured that your good judgment and keen eye will be invaluable.

As you offer comments or ask questions, keep the following in mind:

- Be encouraging and phrase your comments in a positive way. Many people feel uncomfortable talking about themselves and their accomplishments, so be sure to put the job hunter at ease by being a good listener and complimenting his or her answers. Likewise, being constructive in your criticisms will create a better working relationship.

- Don't hesitate to probe. If you do not understand something the job hunter has said or written, ask for an explanation. Why? Because the employer who will be reading the resume is likely to be confused, too, if the same words make their way into the final version of the resume.

- Make sure the job hunter does not sell himself short. Job hunters too often preedit their experiences because they want to get everything down on one page, which is not necessary. Your job is to ask questions that will draw out specifics, particularly numbers that will give the job task or accomplishment a context in which to be better understood.

- Take notes. It's difficult for the job hunter to write while speaking, so as you listen, jot down key words and phrases that sound important to you. Another possibility: Tape-record your question and answer session so that you can replay answers to questions as needed.

- Direct the conversation. Part of your job is to keep the interview on track. Don't let the job hunter stray from the question you've asked; simply say, "That's good information, but save it for later because I'll be asking about it." And keep in mind that no answer should be too long-winded. If you allow the job hunter to digress, you won't be able to produce a draft of the resume in the 90 minutes allotted.

Coach guidelines are interspersed throughout the book to assist you. Be sure to read them before you begin the work described in each section. The role you are about to play in helping the job hunter is an important one.

ARE YOU AN EXPERT RESUME REVIEWER?

Whether or not you have had the experience of evaluating the resumes of prospective job candidates for a position in your company, you and your coach should take this quiz to find out how good you are at pinpointing resume mistakes both big and small. The more aware you are of the things that weaken a resume, the less likely you are to commit those same sins on your own resume.

If you are creating a resume from scratch, begin by critiquing the resume of James Christoferson on page 9. If you're revising a resume, critique the resume of Christina Edwards on page 13 (You can print out copies of this resume to mark up by using the disk that comes with this book). If you don't have a computer, use a separate piece of paper to write down which words, phrases, graphic elements, or sections you feel are inconsistent, unclear, disorganized, or inconclusive. Jot down a brief explanation as to why. There are a ten mistakes and two major omissions in each of these resumes.

Resume 1—James Christoferson

The mistakes here are listed by category—content, punctuation and grammar, organization, and design. Some are much more important than others, but even the ones that may seem trivial can make a resume look less professional.

Content

1. The words *Resume of* are unnecessary; the format of the information tells you that this is a resume.

2. Christoferson's objective is too general. Because this resume will no doubt only be going out to magazine and book publishers, there's no need for this line of information UNLESS it's more specific.

3. The inclusion of colleges that Christoferson attended but did not receive a degree from (with the exception of the summer program) is not necessary. In

Resume 1—Before

Resume of

James Christoferson, 260 East 84th Street, NY, NY 10028
(212) 555-8911

OBJECTIVE: Entry-level job in publishing

EDUCATION

New York University Summer Publishing Institute, a six-week intensive course in magazine and book publishing, Certificate, July, 1996

SUNY Purchase, B.A., 1996, English

Trinity College, Oxford, England, Summer classes in Renaissance History, 1993

Kenyon College, Gambier, Ohio, Candidate for B.A., 1993–94

Lorain County Community College, Candidate for A.A., 1992–93

Baldwin High School, 1992. Honors student. Sports Editor, The Challenger.

ACTIVITIES

Reporter and columnist, The Collegian, 1994–96

Editor, The Literary Quarterly, 1995–96

Captain and member of the soccer team

Swim team, won regional freestyle event twice

EXPERIENCE

Assistant to Product Manager, Summer, 1995	Pepsico Inc., White Plains, New York, Made copies, answered phones, did library research, typed letters
Sales clerk, Summer, 1994	B. Dalton Books, New York, New York Assisted customers, display work, sales
Swim Instructor, Summers, 1990–92	East Hampton, New York Taught children and adults how to swim

fact, it could work against him because it appears that he could not make up his mind about where to attend college (which may or may not be the case). If you are a college graduate, do not include information about your high school unless there is a chance that an alumnus is a potential employer.

4. The single biggest content weakness is the lack of details under both the Activities and Experience sections. The reader can only guess at Christoferson's level of involvement in what appears to be the student newspaper and literary magazine. And while he is somewhat more specific about his job responsibilities, they come across as being ordinary; there is no mention of any results or accomplishments.

Punctuation and Grammar

1. The acronym SUNY (the second entry under Education) should be spelled out; you cannot assume that every reader of your resume will know to which college an acronym refers.

2. The names of publications should be set off in some way because they are publications.

Organization

1. The dates under the Education section get lost in the text; they should be mentioned up front since descriptions are included along with the name of the college and program.

2. Christoferson should consider adding an Interests section; the information listed there serves as a conversational icebreaker in an interview and gives a prospective employer a glimpse into the kind of person you are.

Design

1. Underlining the identification section does nothing to enhance the look of this resume. Christoferson's name should be placed in a more prominent place and a larger typeface used. And his name, street address, city and state, and phone number should each be on a separate line (to make certain that the information is properly read by a computer).

2. Objective is the one category heading that is not lined up with the others (all should be flush left rather than indented). And, unlike the other headings, it's not italicized. (It should be for consistency.)

3. Overall, the resume is too plain.

A round of applause if you caught the majority of these mistakes; you have a keen eye for resume strengths and weaknesses. Don't worry too much if some of

Resume 1—After

James Christoferson

260 East 84th Street
New York, New York 10028
(212) 555-8911

OBJECTIVE Editorial assistant position with a book publisher

EDUCATION Certificate, July, 1996
New York University Summer Publishing Institute (six-week course in magazine and book publishing)

State University of New York at Purchase, B.A., 1996, English

Trinity College, Oxford, England, Summer classes in Renaissance History, 1993

ACTIVITIES **Reporter and columnist**, 1994–96
The Collegian, weekly college newspaper

- Covered an average of 3 sporting events weekly, resulting in at least 2 stories
- Wrote monthly column, "The Sports Observer," which received second-place in 1996 regional student newspaper competition

Editor, 1995–96
The Literary Quarterly, student-produced quarterly

- Reviewed 75 poem and short story submissions quarterly
- Encouraged student participation by addressing 10 creative writing classes; submissions increased 20 percent

EXPERIENCE **Assistant to Product Manager**, Summer, 1995
Pepsico, Inc., White Plains, New York

- Produced reports and correspondence on Word 5.1 (typing speed 80 wpm)
- Asked to correct grammar and sentence construction in reports and letters I typed after demonstrating my proofreading skills
- Directed telephone calls to appropriate staff member

Sales Associate, B. Dalton Books, New York, New York
Summer, 1994

- Assisted customers in making book selections
- Set up special displays and monitored inventory
- Received employee-of-the-month award three times

Swim Instructor, Private pool, East Hampton, New York
Summers, 1990–92

- Taught approximately 120 children and adults how to swim

INTERESTS Soccer (was captain of university soccer team in 1995–96 season)

Swimming (won first place in regional meets in freestyle event in 1994 and 1995)

these mistakes eluded your eye; each of the weaknesses described here will be explained in much greater detail in the sections ahead.

If this job candidate were to go through the process described in the book, he would be able to create a much more descriptive and convincing resume, such as the one shown on page 11.

Resume 2—Christina Edwards

For this resume, the mistakes are listed as content, organizational, or design mistakes. Some are much more important than others, but even the ones that may seem trivial can make a resume look less professional or polished.

Content

1. The single biggest weakness of this resume is in the Experience section. Christina's Responsibilities come across like job descriptions written by the personnel department; the language is dry and impersonal. Two major sins of omission occur here, too: (1) Edwards has not mentioned even one accomplishment, and (2) she does not use numbers to quantify the scope of her responsibilities or accomplishments.

2. Another content shortfall is the way in which Edwards treated her first job experience—*Prior to 1986*. Perhaps because she felt that it was not marketing related, she used only one line to describe four years of experience. Since she was in a very responsible position (skills that may be a factor in the next job she is considered for), she should have given it more weight by setting up that position the same way she did her later jobs, highlighting a few achievements or tasks.

3. The words *Resume of* are not necessary; the format of the information tells you that this is a resume.

4. The personal interests mentioned are so general that they contribute nothing to the profile of the candidate. An added design problem: This heading does not match the two other major section headings.

Organization

1. The Education section is misplaced. Job hunters who are not recent graduates should almost always lead off with their Experience. An exception: career changers who have just completed an academic program that is a prerequisite for the field they are entering.

2. Specialized Training should precede the college entry under the Education section because it's more recent. If the candidate has taken any sequence of courses that specifically prepared her for her next job, it should be mentioned

Resume 2—Before

Resume of

Christina S. Edwards

222 Woodson Avenue
Liberty, Ohio 44071

Work: (419) 555-7145
Home: (419) 555-6342

EDUCATION

B.A., Marketing, Miami University, Oxford, Ohio, 1982
Specialized Training—15 sales and marketing courses sponsored by my
employer and professional association, 1990—1996

EXPERIENCE

Position: Coordinator, Worldwide Marketing and Advertising
Company: Data Information, Inc.
Location: Toledo, Ohio (419) 555-6000
Reported to: Robert Elswood, Vice President, Marketing
Dates: 9/90—present

Responsibilities: Coordinate worldwide promotions and associated marketing
programs designed to stimulate usage of database network. Obtain data from user
members and regions to track and report results of worldwide promotions.
Interface with promotion, advertising, and public relations agencies and
consultants.

Position: Assistant to Vice President of International Marketing
Company: Data Information, Inc.
Location: Toledo, Ohio (419) 555-6000
Reported to: Jane Melbourne, Vice President, International Marketing
Dates: 6/88—9/90

Responsibilities: Aided and assisted the vice president in development and
implementation of international promotions. Researched and prepared external
communications including memos, slide presentations and brochures. Tracked
and monitored all budget expenditures for compliance and variance analysis.

Position: Marketing Representative
Company: Research Software Ventures
Location: Cincinnati, Ohio (513) 555-1100
Reported to: Michael Casa, Marketing Manager
Dates: 1/86—5/88

Responsibilities: Developed and serviced fifty clients. Wrote and produced sales
presentations. Promoted from secretary to marketing rep within six months.

Prior to 1986, I worked as the administrator of a family business, a nursing
home, which was sold in 1985.

Personal Interests: Sports, travel, music.

by name. An additional point: Resist the temptation to highlight information or a heading that appears once, as Christine did by using asterisks before and after Specialized Training.

Design

1. The decision to use the headings—Position, Employer, Location, Reported To, Dates, and Responsibilities—cluttered up the resume. The Reported To heading and category and the phone number listed on the "Location" line can be deleted; that information belongs on a sheet listing references.

2. The Responsibilities section is hard to read because it is a block of copy. It would be more graphically pleasing if the candidate had indented each responsibility or used bullets or another graphic element to separate each responsibility within the block.

3. "Christina S. Edwards" is in a disproportionately large typeface. It should be no more than two point sizes larger than the rest of the type.

4. The Experience heading was not underlined. The graphic elements used to distinguish each heading should be consistent. If there is any possibility that your resume may be scanned by a computer, however, it's best not to underline.

Congratulations if you caught the majority of these mistakes. If you didn't, you'll learn more about resumes strengths and weaknesses throughout the book.

Page 15 shows what Christina S. Edwards' resume looked like after she went through the 90-minute process.

Resume 2—After

Christina S. Edwards

222 Woodson Avenue   Work (419) 555-7145
Liberty, Ohio 44071   Home (419) 555-6342

WORK EXPERIENCE

Data Information, Inc., Toledo, Ohio, June, 1990 to present

Coordinator, Worldwide Marketing and Advertising, September, 1995 to present

- Coordinate five worldwide promotions and associated marketing programs that have increased usage of database network 20 percent since January, 1996
- Designed system to obtain data from user members and regions to track and report amount of usage; information has become instrumental in developing new sales strategies
- Proposed tripling advertising budget; plan accepted by senior management (March, 1996), which helped boost database into top three services nationwide (June, 1996)

Assistant to Vice President of International Marketing, June, 1988 to June, 1990

- Assisted in development and implementation of three international promotions
- Researched and prepared copy and visuals for twenty multimedia presentations and ten sales brochures; twice received letters of commendation from director of sales for these efforts
- Tracked and monitored department budget expenditures of $500,000 after one year on job because "she is a financial whiz and a person of great integrity," (job performance report)

Research Software Ventures, Cincinnati, Ohio, January, 1986 to May, 1988

Marketing Representative

- Expanded list of clients from thirty to fifty in one year's time
- Wrote and produced sales presentations, which management decided to have all reps use because of their effectiveness
- Promoted from secretary to marketing rep within six months.

Golden Acres Nursing Home, Toledo, Ohio, September, 1982 to November, 1985

Administrator

- Assumed operating responsibility for this 100-bed facility (a family-owned business) after having worked in various part-time and summer positions there for eight years
- Supervised construction of building addition (adding twenty beds) and modernizing kitchen and bathrooms
- Added two professional positions to existing three, upgrading therapy and recreational services to patients; received commendation from State Supervisory Board

EDUCATION

Professional training: 15 sales and marketing courses sponsored by my employer and professional association, 1990–1996

B.A., Marketing, Miami University, Oxford, Ohio, 1982

INTERESTS

Marathon running (have completed 10 marathons in five countries)

Listening to and collecting 1940s big band jazz

BEFORE YOU START

Before you sit down with your coach to begin the 90-minute resume process, it's a good idea to gather the materials you will need to work with and prepare a few things that are necessary for smooth sailing during your time together. A list of these materials follows in the box below.

Tools of the Trade

The following list of items are necessary, or in some cases, recommended, for your resume session.

- Several pens or pencils

- Two copies of your current resume (if you have one)

- Photocopies of:

Work Experience Fact Sheet (pp. 21–22)	Job Target/Job Tasks (p. 40)
Skills Fact Sheet (p. 25)	Rate Prospective Job Options (p. 43)
Education Fact Sheet (pp. 28–29)	Work Experience Evaluation Checklist (p. 46)
Activities Fact Sheet (pp. 34–35)	Transferable Skills Worksheet (p. 59)
Interests Fact Sheet (p. 36)	Resume Copy Checklist (pp. 94–96)

(OR use the disk that comes with the book to print out these pages)

- A typewriter or (better yet) a computer (optional)

- A tape recorder and a blank 60-minute cassette (optional)

2 ▶ FIRST, YOUR FACT SHEETS

By preparing fact sheets in advance of working with your coach, you can help your coach phrase questions and move through the interview more quickly. You can use the disk that comes with this book to generate your fact sheets. If you don't have a computer, reproduce one or more copies of the templates that appear after the sample fact sheet in each of the four areas—work experience, education, activities, and interests. If you are creating a resume from scratch, you can skip the next paragraph.

WORK EXPERIENCE FACT SHEET

If you are revising your resume, you will want to at least fill out a Work Experience Fact Sheet so that you can include your current position and any previous jobs that do not appear on your current resume. With it, your coach will be better able to interview you about what you did and accomplished on those jobs. It's probably not necessary for you to prepare other fact sheets (the information may already be on your resume). But if you're a parent who is returning to the workforce after having stayed home to care for your children for a number of years, you may have volunteer experiences that you want to add to an activities fact sheet (your stint as president of the PTA or your contributions to setting up computers and integrating them into the classrooms of your children's school, for example).

For each job you've held, starting with the most recent, fill in the information for which each prompt asks. In addition to full-time positions, include internships, summer jobs (if you're a student or recent graduate), and part-time and unpaid job experiences.

Use the disk that comes with this book to generate a Work Experience Fact Sheet. Or make a copy of pages 21–22.

Sample for First-Time Resume Writer

WORK EXPERIENCE FACT SHEET

Experience 1 (most recent)

Your job title: Assistant to the Program Coordinator

Name of employer: Center for Continuing Education, Capitol University

City, State (where employer located):   Columbus, Ohio

Brief description of business: Offered noncredit courses to community residents

Dates of employment: 1/96–6/96

Experience 2

Your job title: Peer counselor

Name of Employer: Undergraduate English Association, Capitol University

City, State (where employer located):   Columbus, Ohio

Brief description of business: Student organization

Dates of employment: 9/95–6/96 (5 hours a week)

Experience 3

Your job title: Financial Aid Clerk

Name of employer: Financial Aid Services, Capitol University

City, State (where employer located):   Columbus, Ohio

Brief description of business: Processing and awarding of financial aid to
students

Dates of employment: 9/95–12/95

Experience 4

Your job title: Receptionist

Name of employer: The Mandell Agency

City, State (where employer located):   Cleveland, Ohio

Brief description of business: Stock brokerage firm

Dates of employment: Summers, 1993–95

Experience 5

Your job title: Assistant to Art Therapist

Name of employer: St. John's Pediatric Hospital

City, State (where employer located):   Columbus, Ohio

Brief description of business: Health-care facility for children

Dates of employment: 9/94–6/95 (5 hours a week)

Sample for Resume Reviser

If you're adding your most recent job experiences, you may also want to answer two additional prompts: Job Responsibilities and Accomplishments. Try to write at least three entries for each.

WORK EXPERIENCE FACT SHEET

Experience 1 (most recent)

Your job title: Account Executive

Name of employer: AT&T

City, State (where employer located): New York, NY

Brief description of business: Communications provider

Dates of employment: 6/94–present

Job responsibilities:

- Created direct mail/direct response campaigns
- Initiated special programs to increase territory sales leads
- Conceived, produced, and implemented a branch newsletter

Accomplishments:

- Ranked top 10% in nation by attaining 165% of sales objective
- DMDR campaigns averaged 3% return
- Nominated to lead the Manhattan Customer Satisfaction Council

Experience 2

Your job title: Account Executive

Name of employer: Jane Harbour Associates

City, State (where employer located): Stamford, Connecticut

Brief description of business: Public Relations Firm

Dates of employment: 6/92–8/94

Job responsibilities:

- Developed strategy to maximize client exposure
- Wrote press releases; targeted appropriate media contacts
- Worked on preliminary design of newsletter for 2 clients

Accomplishments:

- Handled two of agency's top ten clients at clients' request
- Brought in 5 new clients during my tenure
- Placed 150 client stories in newspapers, magazines, radio, and TV

Experience 3

Your job title: Public Relations Associate

Name of employer: Boston College

City, State (where employer located):   Chestnut Hill, MA

Brief description of business: Four-year private college

Dates of employment: 5/89–4/92

Job responsibilities:

- Developed story ideas about faculty research, departments, and academic issues

- Wrote press releases

- Contacted local and national media

Accomplishments:

- Produced 50-minute slide show on student and faculty research projects

- Promoted from assistant to associate in one year based on successful placement of stories

WORK EXPERIENCE FACT SHEET

Experience 1 (most recent)

Your job title: _____

Name of employer: _____

City, State (where employer located): _____

Brief description of business: _____

Dates of employment: _____

Job responsibilities:

_____

_____

_____

Accomplishments:

_____

_____

_____

Experience 2

Your job title: _____

Name of employer: _____

City, State (where employer located): _____

Brief description of business: _____

Dates of employment: _____

Job responsibilities:

_____

_____

_____

Accomplishments:

_____

_____

_____

Experience 3

Your job title: _____

Name of employer: _____

City, State (where employer located): _____

Brief description of business: _____

Dates of employment: _____

Job responsibilities:

_____

_____

_____

Accomplishments:

_____

_____

_____

Experience 4

Your job title: _____

Name of employer: _____

City, State (where employer located): _____

Brief description of business: _____

Dates of employment: _____

Job responsibilities:

_____

_____

_____

Accomplishments:

_____

_____

_____

Experience 5

Your job title: _____

Name of employer: _____

City, State (where employer located): _____

Brief description of business: _____

Dates of employment: _____

Job responsibilities:

_____

_____

_____

Accomplishments:

_____

_____

_____

SKILLS FACT SHEET

The work experience section of your resume tells an employer what you have done and where you have worked. But it doesn't necessarily reveal what you can do. The more clearly you showcase your skills on your resume, the easier it will be for prospective employers to determine how well your strengths match the needs of the job. This is important in all fields but particularly if you're in a technical field such as engineering or computer technology, as well as in many health-care, clerical and administrative, and financial jobs.

It's a good idea to complete the Skills Fact Sheet whether you're revising your resume or creating your first one. You may want to include your skills in a summary section at the top of your resume or in a separate skills section.

The more you can define and quantify your skills for the employer, the better. One of the blanks in the Skills Fact Sheet asks for proficiency level. You should choose a word or two that best describe how well you can perform the skill. Here are some suggestions: Mastery, Competence, Course Work.

Before you begin filling in your Skills Fact Sheet, review the sample that follows. (Note: Most of the skills listed in it are the names of computer languages or software programs.)

Use the disk that comes with this book to generate a copy of the Skills Fact Sheet. Or copy page 25.

What Qualifies As A Skill?

Anything that you are familiar with or have a mastery of that will be meaningful to an employer is worth mentioning on your resume. Here is a partial list of skills:

- Software programs (note the version of the program you use)
- Type of computers you can use
- Keyboarding (note your words-per-minute speed)
- Accounting
- Writing/editing/copyediting (specify type, for example, technical writing, catalog copy, advertising copy)
- Research (note processes, data-bases, and programs you're familiar with)
- Laboratory processes and procedures
- Test administration and interpretation
- Languages

Sample
SKILLS FACT SHEET

Skill 1: ___HTML___

Proficiency level: ___Competence___

Length of time using skill (number of years/months): ___18 months___

Last used the skill (month/year): ___Current___

Context in which skill used: ___Create Web pages for clients___

Continuing education/training: _____

Certification or license: _____

Skill 2: ___Photoshop___

Proficiency level: ___Master___

Length of time using skill (number of years/months): ___3 years___

Last used the skill (month/year): ___Current___

Context in which skill used: ___Creating ads for clients___

Continuing education/training: _____

Certification or license: _____

Skill 3: ___Quark XPress___

Proficiency level: ___Competence___

Length of time using skill (number of years/months): ___2 years___

Last used the skill (month/year): ___Current___

Context in which skill used: ___Creating ads for clients___

Continuing education/training: ___2 courses—Center for Electronic Arts (95-96)___
Certification or license: _____

Skill 4: ___Spanish___

Proficiency level: ___Fluent/can read and write language___

Length of time using skill (number of years/months): ___10 years___

Last used the skill (month/year): ___Current___

Context in which skill used: ___Teach conversational Spanish course___

Continuing education/training: _____

Certification or license: _____

Skill 5: ___3D Studio___

Proficiency level: ___Course work___

Length of time using skill (number of years/months): ___6 months___

Last used the skill (month/year): ___Current___

Context in which skill used: ___Class projects in game animation___

Continuing education/training: ___In third course (8 sessions/40 lab hours each)___

Certification or license: _____

SKILLS FACT SHEET

Skill 1: _____

Proficiency level: _____

Length of time using skill (number of years/months): _____

Last used the skill (month/year): _____

Context in which skill used: _____

Continuing education/training: _____

Certification or license: _____

Skill 2: _____

Proficiency level: _____

Length of time using skill (number of years/months): _____

Last used the skill (month/year): _____

Context in which skill used: _____

Continuing education/training: _____

Certification or license: _____

Skill 3: _____

Proficiency level: _____

Length of time using skill (number of years/months): _____

Last used the skill (month/year): _____

Context in which skill used: _____

Continuing education/training: _____

Certification or license: _____

Skill 4: _____

Proficiency level: _____

Length of time using skill (number of years/months): _____

Last used the skill (month/year): _____

Context in which skill used: _____

Continuing education/training: _____

Certification or license: _____

Skill 5: _____

Proficiency level: _____

Length of time using skill (number of years/months): _____

Last used the skill (month/year): _____

Context in which skill used: _____

Continuing education/training: _____

Certification or license: _____

EDUCATION FACT SHEET

If you are revising your resume and have no new educational experiences to add, you may want to skip ahead to the Activities Fact Sheet section, which starts on page 30 (or to Chapter 3: Develop A Job Target, on page 37) unless you want to add recent educational experiences to your resume.

If you're creating your first resume, the next fact sheet to prepare is your Education Fact Sheet. You can use the disk that comes with this book to generate an Education Fact Sheet. Or make a copy of pages 28–29.

Sample

EDUCATION FACT SHEET

Most recent college or educational institution attended:

Name of institution: San Francisco State University

City, State (where institution located):   San Francisco, California

Type of degree or certificate received: Bachelor of Arts (B.A.)

Date (including month and year) degree/certificate received: 6/96

Dates of attendance (if degree/certificate not earned):

Program of study (major/minor):   History (major), Political Science (minor)

Grade or grade point average (if B or better):   3.5

Honors or special academic recognition: Cum laude

Scholarships, tuition aid awarded, or percent of education you paid for: Earned 50% of total college expenses through summer and part-time jobs

Other post-high school educational experiences:

Name of institution: Center for Cross-Cultural Study

City, State (where institution located):   Seville, Spain

Type of degree or certificate received:

Date (including month and year) degree/certificate received:

Dates of attendance (if degree/certificate not earned):   Summer, 1995

Program of study (major/minor):   Language, reading, and writing courses

Grade or grade point average (if B or better):

Honors or special academic recognition:

Scholarships, tuition aid rewarded, or percent of education you paid for:

Name of institution: Foothill College

City, State (where institution located): Los Altos Hills, California

Type of degree or certificate received: Associate of Arts (A.A.)

Date (including month and year) degree/certificate received: 6/94

Dates of attendance (if degree/certificate not earned): _____

Program of study (major/minor): Liberal arts

Grade or grade point average (if B or better): 3.2

Honors or special academic recognition: _____

Scholarships, tuition aid awarded, or percent of education you paid for: Paid
for 25% of my expenses through summer and part-time jobs

High school record:

Name of high school: Gunn High School

City, State (where institution located): Palo Alto, California

Date (including month and year) of graduation: 6/92

Dates of attendance (if degree/certificate not earned): _____

Grade or grade point average (if B or better): 3.0

Honors, scholarships, or special academic recognition: _____

EDUCATION FACT SHEET

Most recent college or educational institution attended:

Name of institution: _____

City, State (where institution located): _____

Type of degree or certificate received: _____

Date (including month and year) degree/certificate received: _____

Dates of attendance (if degree/certificate not earned): _____

Program of study (major/minor): _____

Grade or grade point average (if B or better): _____

Honors or special academic recognition: _____

Scholarships, tuition aid rewarded, or percent of education you paid for: _____

Other post-high school educational experiences:

Name of institution: _____

City, State (where institution located): _____

Type of degree or certificate received: _____

Date (including month and year) degree/certificate received: _____

Dates of attendance (if degree/certificate not earned): _____

Program of study (major/minor): _____

Grade or grade point average (if B or better): _____

Honors or special academic recognition: _____

Scholarships, tuition aid rewarded, or percent of education you paid for: _____

Name of institution: _____

City, State (where institution located): _____

Type of degree or certificate received: _____

Date (including month and year) degree/certificate received: _____

Dates of attendance (if degree/certificate not earned): _____

Program of study (major/minor): _____

Grade or grade point average (if B or better): _____

Honors or special academic recognition: _____

Scholarships, tuition aid rewarded, or percent of education you paid for: _____

High school record:

Name of high school: _____

City, State (where institution located): _____

Date (including month and year) of graduation: _____

Dates of attendance (if degree/certificate not earned): _____

Grade or grade point average (if B or better): _____

Honors, scholarships, or special academic recognition: _____

ACTIVITIES FACT SHEET

An activities section is optional, but it can boost your ratings as a candidate, particularly if you played more important roles in campus or community organizations than you did in your summer or part-time jobs.

If you have been involved in controversial social or political activities—for example, a pro-life or pro-choice group—it's better to omit that involvement unless you are planning on applying for jobs with employers who you are confident would value that involvement. If you're not sure where a prospective employer stands on the issue, it could interfere with you being considered for the job.

(Note: If the activities you were involved in are related to the job you hope to land, you may want to list them under your Work Experience section.)

You can use the disk that comes with this book to generate a copy of the Activities Fact Sheet. Or make a copy of pages 34–35.

Sample for First-Time Resume Writer

ACTIVITIES FACT SHEET

Job-related experience 1:

Name of group/organization/activity/team: New York City marathon

Type of involvement (member, secretary, cochair, etc.):   Assistant to
marketing director, New York Road Runners Club

Nature of activity (if not obvious from above):   Advertising and promotion
of the NYC marathon

Dates of involvement: 1/95–11/95

Special recognition you received: One of ten volunteers cited for hours
devoted to marketing success of the marathon

Job-related experience 2:

Name of group/organization/activity/team: USA/Mobil Track and Field
Championship

Type of involvement (member, secretary, cochair, etc.):   Office volunteer

Nature of activity (if not obvious from above):   Prepared for June event

Dates of involvement: 1/94–6/94

Special recognition you received:

Job-related experience 3:

Name of group/organization/activity/team: NYU Marketing Association

Type of involvement (member, secretary, cochair, etc.):   Social chair

Nature of activity (if not obvious from above):

Dates of involvement: 9/93–6/95

Special recognition you received:

Additional activity 1:

Name of group/organization/activity/team: Phi Sigma Kappa

Type of involvement (member, secretary, cochair, etc.):   Intramural chairman

Nature of activity (if not obvious from above):   Social fraternity

Dates of involvement: 1992–1996

Special recognition you received: In the 1995–96 school year, named most
valuable intramural chairman

Additional activity 2:

Name of group/organization/activity/team: ___WNYU Radio___

Type of involvement (member, secretary, cochair, etc.): ___Sports announcer___

Nature of activity (if not obvious from above): _____

Dates of involvement: ___1992–93___

Special recognition you received: _____

Additional activity 3:

Name of group/organization/ activity/team: ___NYU Development Office___

Type of involvement (member, secretary, cochair, etc.): ___Phonathon volunteer___

Nature of activity (if not obvious from above): _____

Dates of involvement: ___March, 1995 and 1996___

Special recognition you received: ___Received certificate for raising more than___ ___$10,000 through phone solicitations of alumni___

Sample for Parent Returning to Work Force
ACTIVITIES FACT SHEET

Job-related experience 1:

Name of group/organization/activity/team: Parents of Children with
Learning Disabilities

Type of involvement (member, secretary, cochair, etc.):   President (1995–96)

Nature of activity (if not obvious from above):   Work with school district to
provide high-quality services to children with learning disabilities and
to lobby state and federal legislators for funds to support programs

Dates of involvement: 1990–96

Special recognition you received: Cited for innovative ideas for funding by
regional educators group, 1996

Job-related experience 2:

Name of group/organization/activity/team: Parents Education Committee,
Hillcrest School

Type of involvement (member, secretary, cochair, etc.):   Cochair (1994–95)

Nature of activity (if not obvious from above):   Identified speakers for six
annual programs for parents of students

Dates of involvement: 1993–95

Special recognition you received: Highest attendance ever recorded in
committee's ten-year history during year I served as cochair

Job-related experience 3:

Name of group/organization/ activity/team: Hillcrest Parent PTA

Type of involvement (member, secretary, cochair, etc.):   Phonathon volunteer

Nature of activity (if not obvious from above):   Solicited contributions from
parents during annual fund-raising drive

Dates of involvement: 1990–95

Special recognition you received: Solicited pledges totaling over $20,000 over
five-year period

ACTIVITIES FACT SHEET

Job-related experience 1:

Name of group/organization/activity/team: _____

_____

Type of involvement (member, secretary, cochair, etc.): _____

Nature of activity (if not obvious from above): _____

_____

_____

Dates of involvement: _____

Special recognition you received: _____

_____

Job-related experience 2:

Name of group/organization/activity/team: _____

_____

Type of involvement (member, secretary, cochair, etc.): _____

Nature of activity (if not obvious from above): _____

_____

_____

Dates of involvement: _____

Special recognition you received: _____

_____

Job-related experience 3:

Name of group/organization/activity/team: _____

_____

Type of involvement (member, secretary, cochair, etc.): _____

Nature of activity (if not obvious from above): _____

_____

Dates of involvement: _____

Special recognition you received: _____

_____

Additional activity 1:

Name of group/organization/activity/team: _____

_____

Type of involvement (member, secretary, cochair, etc.): _____

Nature of activity (if not obvious from above): _____

_____

_____

Dates of involvement: _____

Special recognition you received: _____

_____

Additional activity 2:

Name of group/organization/activity/team: _____

_____

Type of involvement member, secretary, cochair, etc.): _____

Nature of activity (if not obvious from above): _____

_____

_____

Dates of involvement: _____

Special recognition you received: _____

_____

Additional activity 3:

Name of group/organization/activity/team: _____

_____

Type of involvement (member, secretary, cochair, etc.): _____

Nature of activity (if not obvious from above): _____

_____

_____

Dates of involvement: _____

Special recognition you received: _____

_____

INTERESTS FACT SHEET

An interests section is also optional. Unless you're a couch potato, it's a good idea to include it. Employers who plan to interview you often appreciate knowing what your interests and involvements outside of work are because it provides insight into the kind of person you are. Interviewers often start off with questions from this section. If you and a prospective boss share similar interests, it can help you clinch the job. For now it's fine to jot down short list of activities you enjoy doing in your free time on your interests fact sheet. You can decide which ones to keep on your final resume later on. Use the disk that comes with this book to print out an Interests Fact Sheet. Or make a copy of the following.

Sample
INTERESTS FACT SHEET

Hobbies: ___Surfing the Internet___

Sports you play, coach, or teach: ___Windsurfing___

Community, civic, or school involvement (that you don't plan to mention elsewhere):
___Rotary Club Member___

Volunteer work—name of organization/type of involvement (that you don't plan to mention elsewhere): ___Reader for the blind___

Types of books/magazines you like to read: ___Contemporary biographies___

Other: ___Collecting antiques___

INTERESTS FACT SHEET

Hobbies: _____

Sports you play, coach, or teach: _____

Community, civic, or school involvement (that you don't plan to mention elsewhere):

_____

Volunteer work—name of organization/type of involvement (that you don't plan to mention elsewhere): _____

_____

Types of books/magazines you like to read: _____

Other: _____

3 ▶ DEVELOP A JOB TARGET

Now that you've filled out your fact sheets, your second advance task is to write down your job target—that is, describe the position you would like to land. The more focused you are about what you want to do and the more knowledgeable you are about the responsibilities of that job and the skills required, the easier it will be for you to develop a resume that will attract the attention of employers for whom you want to work.

Whether or not you intend to use a job objective on your resume, you should write one for you and your interviewer to use as a basis for making decisions about which skills and experiences to emphasize.

That's true whether you are creating a resume from scratch or updating a resume. "We urge all of our clients to start revising their resumes by coming up with a job objective," says Richard J. Chagnon, a senior vice president with Right Associates, a worldwide outplacement firm headquartered in Philadelphia. "The reason? It forces you to think not only in terms of what you have done but what you can do."

The more specific and realistic your job objective, the easier it will be to make choices about what to include and exclude from your resume.

Sample Target—For First-Time Job Hunters

If you majored in communications and have worked as an intern for television programs, your job objective might be:

● A production assistant for a news or documentary television program

This job hunter's particular interest in news and documentary programming is a focal point around which to build those aspects of his or her experience and skills that will support that ambition.

Sample Target—For Job Hunters with Experience

The job target of a certified public accountant with international tax experience who has been in a nonmanagement position might be:

- To work as an international tax specialist in a position that would involve making recommendations on strategic planning issues and helping senior managers make financial policy decisions

In this case, the job hunter's interest in making a contribution to strategic planning and financial decision making can be useful benchmarks in highlighting those aspects of his or her experience and skills that attest to his or her ability to step into that role.

Having more than one job target is not a problem. Whether you are a recent graduate (who cannot decide among several interesting job options) or a job hunter with experience, you can increase your odds of landing interviews if you're willing to consider several types of related positions or industries. If that's the case, you will probably also want to create different versions of your resumes, each of which emphasizes aspects of your skills or experience that support that job target.

Next, based on what you know about your target job, write down at least four or five tasks for which someone in that position would be responsible. Why? It will enable you to make better judgments about what to emphasize from your past jobs or academic experiences. You can use the Job Target/Job Tasks Worksheet on page 40 (again, you may want to make several copies of this), or use the disk that comes with this book to generate copies.

The third step is to identify the two, three, or four areas of expertise under which these job tasks would fit. The benefit of doing this analysis is that it provides a basis for you and your interviewer to analyze how your past academic and work experiences mesh with your job target.

If you have never before thought about how to group like sets of skills under a larger heading, the box on page 41 can help you. It does not contain all areas of expertise (that list would include hundreds of entries). But by looking over the action verbs listed under each area of expertise, you will get a better idea of how skills can be organized under areas of expertise (They are sometimes referred to as functions or functional headings and used as the main section headings in functional resumes—that is, resumes that are organized by area of expertise).

Sample 1
Job Target/Job Tasks

Job Objective: A position as an exercise physiologist at a health club

Job Tasks:

1.   Evaluate clients' fitness capabilities
2.   Design physical fitness improvement program suited to clients' needs
3.   Train clients in equipment use and monitor client progress
4.   Teach weight-training techniques and aerobic classes
5.   Encourage and motivate clients to stick with fitness routines

Areas of Expertise:

Evaluation, instruction, and communication

Sample 2
Job Target/Job Tasks

Job Objective: Work in a corporate office environment as an industrial hygienist

Job Tasks:

1.   Monitor ventilation, lighting, or other work conditions to ensure employee health and safety
2.   Collect samples of dust or other toxic materials for analysis
3.   Educate employees about on-the-job health hazards and preventive measures
4.   Review processes that expose employees to noise, chemicals, or biological hazards
5.   Write up findings and recommendations clearly, concisely, and persuasively

Areas of Expertise:

Investigation, education, and communication

JOB TARGET/JOB TASKS

Target 1

Job Objective: _____

Job Tasks:

1. _____
2. _____
3. _____
4. _____
5. _____

Areas of expertise:

_____

Target 2

Job Objective: _____

Job Tasks:

1. _____
2. _____
3. _____
4. _____
5. _____

Areas of expertise:

_____

Target 3

Job Objective: _____

Job Tasks:

1. _____
2. _____
3. _____
4. _____
5. _____

Areas of expertise:

_____

Areas of Expertise

Accounting	Administration	Advertising	Coaching
Plan	Administer	Create	Train
Audit	Direct	Write	Coordinate
Calculate	Organize	Design	Instruct
Review	Program	Conceptualize	Direct
Analyze	Oversee	Develop	Schedule
Project	Manage	Formulate	Organize
Estimate	Control	Plan	Lead
Examine	Institute	Negotiate	Motivate

Communications	Design	Finance	Fund-Raising
Interview	Create	Leverage	Propose
Write	Lay out	Research	Solicit
Present	Conceptualize	Analyze	Contact
Edit	Develop	Formulate	Write
Conceptualize	Illustrate	Diagnose	Develop
Develop	Render	Compile	
Outline		Calculate	
Research		Negotiate	

Management	Personnel	Public Relations	Research
Control	Screen	Promote	Investigate
Administer	Interview	Develop	Study
Supervise	Evaluate	Research	Test
Analyze	Analyze	Write	Analyze
Implement	Administer	Market	Calculate
Direct	Test		Solve
			Determine

UNDECIDED ABOUT WHAT TO DO?
TRY THE BALANCE SHEET APPROACH

If you are not sure what kind of first job you want, you should research your options. There are many ways to do that, among them talking to people in your field whose judgment you trust, taking a short course in making career decisions (many are offered through college placement or career planning offices) or going the self-help route with a career decision-making book such as *Starting Out, Starting Over: Finding the Work That's Waiting for You* by Linda Peterson (Davies-Black Publishing).

If you cannot decide among your options, try the balance sheet approach to making a decision. The concept is easy: You rate the things that are most important to you about a job and give each factor a numerical value. By adding up the score, you can determine which option is your top choice.

Start by making a list of all the possibilities you are entertaining. Then, beginning with the first one on your list, assign a weight (on a scale of one to five, five being the best rating) to the factors that influence each job's appeal. You can use the form on page 43 (or print it out using the disk that comes with this book).

RATING YOUR JOB OPTIONS

After filling in each prospective job option, assign a value of 1 to 5 to each of the factors that follow. Here's what each numerical value means:

> 5 = Almost certain to be the case
> 4 = Very likely
> 3 = Somewhat likely
> 2 = Less likely
> 1 = Almost certain not to be the case

Total up the points for each job and then compare the totals. The jobs that get the highest points are your best bets for your next position.

RATE PROSPECTIVE JOB OPTIONS

Name of job 1: _____

Salary will meet your needs/expectations _____

You will have control over your work (what you do/when you do it) _____

The hours are likely to meet your needs _____

Good potential for advancement _____

Job security (or enough to suit you) _____

Interesting/challenging job responsibilities _____

Desirable job environment _____

Other factor important to you _____ _____

    Total the points _____

Name of job 2: _____

Salary will meet your needs/expectations _____

You will have control over your work (what you do/when you do it) _____

The hours are likely to meet your needs _____

Good potential for advancement _____

Job security (or enough to suit you) _____

Interesting/challenging job responsibilities _____

Desirable job environment _____

Other factor important to you _____ _____

    Total the points _____

Name of job 3: _____

Salary will meet your needs/expectations _____

You will have control over your work (what you do/when you do it) _____

The hours are likely to meet your needs _____

Good potential for advancement _____

Job security (or enough to suit you) _____

Interesting/challenging job responsibilities _____

Desirable job environment _____

Other factor important to you _____ _____

    Total the points _____

4 ▶ READY, SET, START THE INTERVIEW

N ow that your preliminary work is done, it's time to call in your coach and start the clock. If you have a computer, print out the questions and coach guidelines that go with each set of fact sheets so your coach can review them in advance and refer to them easily during the interview.

STEP 1
IS YOUR JOB TARGET ON TARGET?

 Time for this exercise: 5 minutes
Total elapsed time: none

The first step in the process is to talk about your job target and its tasks so that your interviewer can ask better questions and help you judge what belongs in your resume. Be open to your coach's comments and suggestions; he or she may bring up points that have not occurred to you and that may be convincing reasons why you might want to alter your job target—or add additional job targets.

> *Coach Guideline: Evaluate the job target. Is it clearly stated? Is it too narrow? too broad? If the resume is being revised, does it make sense given the job hunter's current or previous job? Are the tasks and areas of expertise of the job target analyzed correctly? Note: You may not be able to judge this accurately unless you have more experience in the target field than the job hunter does.*

Start the clock, and begin talking. You have 5 minutes. When you've finished, skip ahead to Step 3: The Interview (page 47) if you're creating a new resume. If you're revising your resume, continue with the next step.

STEP 2
CRITIQUE YOUR CURRENT RESUME

Time for this exercise: 20 minutes
Total elapsed time: 25 minutes

What to do beforehand: Have two copies of your current resume on hand, along with two copies of the Work Experience Evaluation Checklist on page 46 (you can print out copies using the disk that comes with this book).

Your second task is to jointly evaluate the most critical section on your resume—your Work Experience section. It's very important to be able to see a thread of connection from one job to another. If employers can see the connection between customers, the type of product, their territory, marketing experience, or whatever, they get the sense that the candidate controlled his or her career rather than the other way around. And that's an important factor in their selecting one candidate over another.

Critiquing your work experience section can give both you and your coach a better idea about what to work on during the interview. Both of you should have copies of your current resume and the Work Experience Evaluation Checklist in front of you. Scan the checklist; your coach should also take a few minutes to read over your resume.

Then, using the questions as a guideline, assess your current resume. You have two options about discussing your reactions: (1) You can go question by question and take turns offering your views (and write down your points of agreement as you go), or (2) you can jot down your comments about each question and then compare notes. Your coach may pick up on things that you cannot see because you created the resume. By discussing the weaknesses of your current resume as each of you sees them, you can better focus your efforts during the interview and writing portion of the 90-minute process.

If you have chosen to go through the checklist separately, either one of you can start the discussion, although your coach may feel more comfortable if you go first. The easiest way to proceed is to work down the resume job by job. If a weakness exists, it probably occurs throughout the work experience section—for example, not including any numbers or accomplishments. Rather than having each of you run through your list of comments, conduct a give-and-take conversation so that you cover the same ground together.

Your goal at the end of this exercise is to identify what needs the most work. It may be the case, for example, that a series of jobs you had at your current place of employment needs consolidating to eliminate repetition. Or you may want to work at developing the connections among your jobs so that your job experience will appear cohesive.

Work Experience Evaluation Checklist

1. Are there a sufficient number of responsibilities under each job?

2. Do the job responsibilities provide enough detail about your skills, knowledge, and expertise?

3. Are there enough job tasks listed that support your new job target (or should more be added)?

4. Is the language of the descriptions clear and concise and does each begin with a strong action verb?

5. Are there numbers and percentages that quantify the scope of your responsibilities?

6. Is there too much repetition of job tasks or action verbs?

7. Are there examples or evidence to back up claims?

8. Have you included descriptions of accomplishments in each job?

9. Are there numbers and percentages or language details to quantify accomplishments?

10. Are dates of employment given for each job listed?

Coach Guideline: Avoid getting bogged down over a small point; if necessary, set it aside for later consideration. As the two of you talk about specific points, keep the following questions in mind:

1. Are job experiences presented in a logical and easy-to-follow way?

2. Do they support the kind of position the job hunter is going after?

3. Are the connections among jobs clear (in other words, are there links between skills, areas of expertise, or industries?)

Put aside the book now, and begin the exercise. You have 20 minutes to critique your resume and discuss its strengths and weaknesses with your coach.

STEP 3
THE INTERVIEW

 Time for this exercise: 15 minutes
Total elapsed time: 40 minutes

It's time for the interview part of the 90-minute process. The point of having the interviewer ask you questions is to have you talk about your work and educational background, which is much easier than writing about it. It's the coach's job to ask, "Explain what you mean," or "Can you give me an example?" if he or she doesn't understand your answer. Try to use words that clearly and simply describe your job responsibilities, skills, and accomplishments. Avoid using jargon or technical terms, and try to make your answers concrete and descriptive.

> *Coach guideline: Keep a pen or pencil in hand at all times; you will want to jot down words, phrases, and well-expressed ideas as the job hunter answers the questions you ask. Taking good notes will make it easier to put together the resume. Better yet, take notes on your computer. You can use the Note Organizer on the disk that comes with this book. Inputting information as you do the interview will save you the time of entering it later. Before moving on to the next question, read back what you have got. Work together to get down a phrase that contains an action word (the way you did this job task), a direct object (who, what), and qualifying clauses (to do or accomplish what).*

> *Example*

> Organized *(action word)*
> volunteers *(direct object)*
> to raise funds for the library *(qualifying clause)*

> *An alternative to taking notes as you go is to use a tape recorder to tape your session. It will allow you to rewind and play back parts of the interview, which can be helpful if something brilliant is said and promptly forgotten. But keep in mind it will ultimately take you more time to tape and listen than it would to take notes as you go.*

While a significant portion of your practice interview may be devoted to work experience, you might also wish to include some discussion of your educational background, interests, and activities. The following four sections show how the information on your Work Experience, Education, Activities, and Interests Fact Sheets can be put to work in an interview and how the interview, in turn, can help you refine your worksheet entries.

QUESTIONS GENERATED FROM THE
WORK EXPERIENCE FACT SHEET

Let's start with the Work Experience Fact Sheet. When answering the interviewer's questions, try to use numbers, percentages, and amounts to describe how many, how often, or how much Quantifying what you have done and what you know helps put your accomplishments and skills into perspective for the employer who will be reviewing your resume. The more specifics you can provide, the easier it is for the employer to understand how you can fit into his or her organization.

Questions

- What exactly did you do on your job on a regular (daily, weekly, monthly) basis? (Encourage the job hunter to name at least five.)

- Can you point to specific results or accomplishments of your work? Describe them and, if possible, quantify them with numbers.

- Can you name one or more important projects you worked on, even if it was only in a support or administrative role? Briefly describe what the project involved, and your role. Were you able to contribute anything above and beyond what your job required you to do?

- Did you suggest an idea that was successfully implemented by your boss, department, or company? Describe what it involved, your role in making it work, and any creditor or compliments you received as a result.

- Do you manage the work of anyone other than yourself? If so, how many people? At what level (clerical, technical, administrative) were those employees?

- Did you train any employees? Describe the processes, procedures or tasks you taught them, and explain whether you did it on your own initiative (or at your boss's request).

- What have you done on the job that has give you satisfaction or won compliments or recognition from your boss, management or clients?

- Have you ever had to handle an emergency or crisis situation? Please describe it.

- Have you ever had to step into the shoes of a more experienced colleague or take over for your boss due to sickness or an emergency? Please describe.

Coach Guideline: You should have the job hunter's fact sheets in front of you. Start with the most recent job and work backward. If the job hunter has already given some thought to what he or she does on the job and what his or her accomplishments have been, you may not need to go beyond the first two questions for each job. The additional questions are suggestions of what to ask if you need to dig deeper. It's crucial, however, to get numbers (whenever possible) and at least one or two accomplishments or results for each job. Remember to spend more time on those jobs that relate to the job target.

If you're working with a job hunter who is revising his or her resume, you may only need to ask questions about the current or most recent job (since you will have already critiqued jobs listed on the resume being revised).

Treat all kinds of work experience—paid, volunteer, part-time, or full-time—the same way. If the job hunter has not had much work experience or experience directly related to the kind of work he or she is applying for, it's particularly important to encourage the person to talk about what he or she has learned and contributed.

Finally, do your best to keep the interview on track and to keep the job hunter from going off on unnecessary tangents.

As you will see from the Sample Conversation that follows, your coach should feel free to ask questions based on answers that you give. If you are not the type of person who talks a lot, you may have to ask a lot of questions, as the coach in the sample conversation does. If you're revising your resume, skip ahead to the second Sample Conversation that begins on page 51.

SAMPLE CONVERSATION 1—WORK EXPERIENCE
(FOR FIRST-TIME RESUME WRITER)

Coach: What exactly did you do as a customer-care representative for ABC long-distance carrier?

Job Hunter: I answered calls from customers and handled any questions or complaints they had.

Coach: How many customer inquiries did you handle in a typical work day?

Job Hunter: The average number of inquiries handled per hour was ten, but my average was fourteen. I received an employee-of-the-month citation five times in the two years I worked for ABC.

Coach: How were you able to handle more calls than other representatives?

Job Hunter: I learned how to listen carefully to what customers were saying. I asked questions and, because I constantly reviewed new pricing policies, was able to either give them the information they needed or resolve their complaint without having to ask my manager for help.

Coach: What was the ratio of informational calls versus complaints?

Job Hunter: Five to one.

Coach: How did you handle complaints?

Job Hunter: I completed a two-week training course on customer relations but developed most of my expertise by trial and error. I discovered that by sympathizing with the caller, explaining how the problem may have occurred and offering to do everything within my power to make sure it didn't happen again, I was able to win customers' confidence.

What to Enter on the
Work Experience Fact Sheet
(UNDER RESPONSIBILITIES AND/OR ACCOMPLISHMENTS)

- Handled fourteen calls from customers per hour, resulting in five citations as employee of the month

- Developed good listening skills

- Learned how to ask the right questions of customers

- Studied changes in company pricing policies so I could explain them to customers

- Developed expertise in handling customers with complaints

SAMPLE CONVERSATION 2—WORK EXPERIENCE
(REVISING A RESUME)

Situation: A job hunter who is currently director of development at a small liberal arts college who hopes to land a job with the same title at a much larger private university.

Coach: What do you do as a director of development?

Job Hunter: I have four major areas of responsibility: (1) coming up with fresh ideas for fund-raising campaigns; (2) maintaining good relationships with benefactors; (3) identifying new potential donors; and (4) managing a staff of five who implemented fund-raising activities.

Coach: How do you maintain good relationships?

Job Hunter: I write personal letters, make phone calls, produce a newsletter, and arrange to see people in their homes or offices.

Coach: How does this job differ from your previous one as a development specialist?

Job Hunter: My main responsibilities as a specialist were implementing other people's ideas, and I managed one clerical employee.

Coach: What kind of results have you had in your current job?

Job Hunter: I created a successful annual fund-raising campaign that we have used for four years. The first year, it increased donations by 10 percent, and that has steadily increased by an average of 5 percent each year since. Our benefactor base has increased by one third.

Coach: Are there any less tangible accomplishments you can claim credit for?

Job Hunter: I introduced incentive plans for the entire staff. Morale is better and turnover down.

Note: This sample is an abbreviated version of how an actual interview or conversation might go. The coach could, for example, ask the job hunter to expand on each of his or her four main areas of responsibilities to get additional details. The coach might also probe for additional results. The question about how the current and previous job differed can help both of you decide how to handle unnecessary repetition of job tasks.

What to Enter on the Work Experience Fact Sheet
(UNDER RESPONSIBILITIES AND/OR ACCOMPLISHMENTS)

- Generating new fund-raising ideas;

  Result: New annual fund-raising campaign—10 percent increase first year, about 5 percent growth last three years

- Maintaining relationships with benefactors: Writing personal letters, making phone calls, producing a newsletter, making in-person visits.

- Identifying new potential donors;

- Managing a five staff;

  Result: Improved morale, reduced turnover

QUESTIONS GENERATED FROM THE EDUCATION FACT SHEET

Let's tackle the education fact sheet next. If you have graduated from school more than ten years ago, and you have no recent education information to add, your coach need only ask a question or two to make sure the information on your existing resume or on your Education Fact Sheet is clear. If you do not need to make any changes, you can move ahead to "Questions Generated from the Activities Fact Sheet" on page 53.

> *Coach Guideline: Start by reading over the information on the Education Fact Sheet. Ask questions about anything that is unclear to you, even if it's a simple detail about the type of degree or certificate received.*

Questions

- Did you work to put yourself through school? If so, for what percentage of your education did you pay?

- How were you selected for the honor, scholarship, or award you've listed? Was it based on grades, leadership ability, or involvement in school organizations?

- Who awarded the honor (faculty, administration, officers of an organization, your peers)?

- Were others selected or were you the only one?

- Was there a cash award or scholarship involved? If so, how much?

SAMPLE CONVERSATION—EDUCATION

Coach: You wrote on your fact sheet that you received an honor for outstanding academic achievement. What exactly did you do?

Job Hunter: I wrote a term paper that was cited as one of the ten best written by a senior.

Coach: What was the subject of your paper?

Job Hunter: The title was "Perspectives on the Vietnam War: Veterans and Families of Those Killed in Action Tell Their Stories." I interviewed five veterans and five families in addition to doing research from print sources.

Coach: How was your paper selected?

Job Hunter: My political science professor nominated it.

Coach: How many other papers were nominated?

Job Hunter: My professor told me it was over 300; all twenty departments in the arts and sciences division competed. A faculty committee made the final selections.

What to Enter on the Education Fact Sheet

- Wrote one of ten best senior term papers entitled "Perspectives on the Vietnam War"

- Nominated for recognition by political science professor

- Selected by a faculty committee from a field of twenty finalists and over 300 applicants

QUESTIONS GENERATED FROM THE ACTIVITIES FACT SHEET

As your coach asks you questions, try to use specifics to describe your involvement in campus or community organizations, sports, or activities.

> **Coach Guideline:** *If the purpose of the organization is not obvious from the name, ask whether it is a social, professional, community, student government, or other special interest group.*

Questions

- What was the nature and extent of your involvement in the group?
- Did you serve on any committees, participate in planning or executing organization projects or do fund-raising? What were the results of your efforts?
- Were you an elected or appointed officer of the club or organization? What were your contributions or accomplishments as an officer?
- Did you develop any skills related to your job target through your participation?

SAMPLE CONVERSATION 1—ACTIVITIES

(RECENT GRADUATE)

Coach: What did you do as the copy editor of the yearbook?

Job Hunter: I wrote the lead articles for each section of the book. I helped the editor-in-chief make story assignments. I edited and proofread those assignments when they came in. I also worked with the art director to come up with a design format using Quark Xpress. I made sure all the copy was input correctly into the computer. And I signed off on all the mechanicals.

Coach: How much time did this involvement require?

Job Hunter: I spent 15 hours a week on it over a period of eight months.

Coach: Did you learn any special skills in this job?

Job Hunter: My copyediting skills improved, particularly because the yearbook adviser is a former newspaper copy desk editor. I knew a bit about desktop publishing, but I mastered the Quark Xpress program during the time I used it.

Coach: Was the yearbook a success?

Job Hunter: We sold a record number of copies. And the yearbook won an award for superior design from the Student Press Association.

What to Enter on the Activities Fact Sheet

- Wrote lead articles for book sections

- Helped assign stories

- Edited and proofread stories

- Worked with art director to design format

- Supervised copy input

- Signed off on mechanicals

- Sharpened copyediting skills with help of adviser

- Mastered Quark XPress

- Helped produce yearbook whose sales surpassed school record; won superior design award from Student Press Association

SAMPLE CONVERSATION 2—ACTIVITIES
(JOB CANDIDATE RETURNING TO WORK FORCE)

Coach: How did you get the assignment of coordinating the study for your town's recreation complex?

Job Hunter: I had successfully managed the campaigns of 3 city council members. They nominated me for this volunteer post because they were familiar with how I work; the city council unanimously approved my appointment.

Coach: What did the assignment involve?

Job Hunter: I was given five months to research and write a report about the scope and cost of building a town recreation complex. The city council provided general guidelines on how much they felt could be spent and what they wanted to the complex to include.

Coach: How did you do the research?

Job Hunter: I visited a half-dozen other complexes around the state comparable to what we wanted. I interviewed the project managers and town administrative personnel to determine costs, pitfalls, and smart ways of accomplishing such a project.

Coach: Can you talk a little bit about the written report?

Job Hunter: It was 25 pages in length, but 10 of those pages were charts and architectural drawings that I used to illustrate different options. I used Excel to do the computations of the costs of each of the three options with three price tags—$4M, $5M, and $6M.

Coach: What was the upshot of your report?

Job Hunter: The city council voted to approve the $5M option, pending approval of a bond issue by the voters, which passed by a 3 to 1 margin the following November. I made over two dozen appearances at various functions around town to help promote and explain the idea. I received a letter from the city council that said that without my efforts, the complex would probably not have become a reality so quickly.

What to Enter on the Activities Fact Sheet

- Appointed by city council to direct recreational complex feasibility study

- Visited half-dozen recreational complexes around state

- Interviewed project managers and city administration about their experiences

- Produced 25-page report on 3 complex options, with $4M, $5M, and $6M price tags

- Middle option approved by city council; voters approved bond to fund it

QUESTIONS GENERATED FROM THE INTERESTS FACT SHEET

You can move through this part of the interview quickly if you first review your Interests Fact Sheet and select the three most important ones to focus on.

Coach Guideline: Aim for specifics about the interests the job hunter has listed and find out whether he or she has only a passing familiarity with them (in which case, they shouldn't be mentioned) or a genuine passion or involvement.

Questions

- What exactly is your involvement with (the interests listed)?
- How much do you know about it?
- How often do you do it?
- Have you ever received any special recognition for your involvement with (the interests listed)?

SAMPLE CONVERSATION—INTERESTS

Coach: What kind of photography do you like to do?

Job Hunter: I like to do photographs of animals that are endangered.

Coach: Where do you go to find these animals?

Job Hunter: I like to photograph them in the wild, and I'm able to make enough money from selling my photos to finance at least one trip per year.

Coach: How many images do you sell a year?

Job Hunter: About 500. I print my own photographs, so I'm able to keep costs down. And by keeping my profit margin low, I can sell them at a price that most people can afford.

What to Enter on the Interests Fact Sheet

- Take photographs of endangered species
- Sell 500 images a year; profits used to finance trips to environments where animals live

Now that you have the basics of doing a good interview down, it's time to start asking questions. When you have completed this exercise (you have 15 minutes), page ahead to Chapter 5, Coming Up with Great Resume Language, on page 63 unless you're changing careers. If that's the case, read "For Career Changers Only: The Matching Game," which follows.

For Career Changers Only: The Matching Game

Time for this exercise: 35 minutes

If you are looking for a job in a new field because you no longer feel challenged or excited about your work or because the demand for people with your skills and experience is shrinking, it's important to carefully think through your approach to finding your next position. The biggest hurdle you must overcome is to convince a potential employer why you are qualified for the job. "The job hunter has to come up with what I call 'instant recognition factors' so that the reader will say, 'It wouldn't hurt to talk to her even though her background is out of the ordinary,'" says John D. Erdlen, president of Strategic Outsourcing, Inc.

What are "instant recognition factors?" They are skills and experiences which are gained in one context (usually a job but also in course work, an avocation or hobby or community or professional activities) but that could be effectively used in another context. These factors are often called transferable skills and experiences.

Once you have identified your transferable skills and experiences, you can record them on the Transferable Skills Worksheet on page 59. Then you can work with your coach to translate these skills into resume copy, as demonstrated by the examples in the following two sections.

Identifying Skills and Experiences in a Work Context

Now it's time to scan your current resume to identify your own transferable skills from work experiences. Some may jump out at you because the action verbs you used to describe job tasks may be the same as or similar to those required in the new career you have targeted; others will be less obvious.

Coach Guideline: Ask the following three questions for any job task that supports your case for making a change to your new career but needs expanding (one that has been checked by the job hunter or you). Be sure to include job tasks from positions not included on your current resume (refer to the Fact Sheets).

1. Explain in more detail what this job task involved.

2. What skills were involved in executing this task?

3. What role did this task play in accomplishing your work objectives?

You and your coach should each work with your copies of your most recent resume and fact sheets. Put check marks next to the job responsibilities and accomplishments that may be evidence that you are qualified to do the work that's an essential part of the job you hope to land.

Example—Transferable Skills From Work Experience

Situation: A high school English teacher hopes to get a job as an instructor in the training and development department of a corporation. The job task on her current resume reads:

—Prepared lesson plans for literature and writing classes for 30 high school seniors

SAMPLE CONVERSATION

Coach: Tell me more about what preparing lesson plans involved.

Career Changer: I developed curriculum outlines by working with the history, social studies and art teachers so that there were links between what each of us was teaching. I tried to come up with interesting ideas for homework assignments that would involve reading and writing skills. I even published the best ones in a weekly newspaper.

Coach: What skills did you use in preparing lesson plans?

Career Changer: It involved analytical skills because it was an interdisciplinary exercise. It involved teamwork. It required imagination and creativity and a practical sense of what would motivate students to work.

Coach: What role did lesson preparation play in your overall teaching responsibilities?

Career Changer: A critical one. Without good planning, I would not have been able to present my own thoughts in a cohesive way. Nor would the students have sensed an order or structure to what they were learning. And that would have affected how attentive they were—and how much they participated in class and in doing their homework assignments.

What to Enter on the Transferable Skills Worksheet

- Developed lesson plans
- Came up with interesting ideas for homework assignments
- Published best papers in class newspaper
- Involved analytical skills and teamwork, imagination, and creativity
- Knowing what would motivate students, keep their attention, and affect participation

Now, start the interview. You will have twenty minutes to complete it.

TRANSFERABLE SKILLS WORKSHEET
Work Experience

Transferable Experience	Resume Copy
1. _____	1. _____
2. _____	2. _____
3. _____	3. _____
4. _____	4. _____
5. _____	5. _____
6. _____	6. _____
7. _____	7. _____
8. _____	8. _____
9. _____	9. _____
10. _____	10. _____

Other Experiences

Transferable Experience	Resume Copy
1. _____	1. _____
2. _____	2. _____
3. _____	3. _____
4. _____	4. _____
5. _____	5. _____
6. _____	6. _____
7. _____	7. _____
8. _____	8. _____
9. _____	9. _____
10. _____	10. _____

IDENTIFYING SKILLS AND EXPERIENCES OUTSIDE OF A JOB CONTEXT

In addition to finding parallels for your impending career change in past job experience, you may also find evidence to support your skills by looking at your involvements beyond your job. They, too, can help you make a case for being a candidate worth considering.

Coach Guideline: Use the five action verbs from the description of the tasks of the targeted job (refer to your answers on page 40) and ask the following questions. If you see a possible connection between an activity that is mentioned on the current resume and a job task from the job hunter's ideal job, ask about it in particular.

Questions

- Did you ever have to (fill in with appropriate action verb) in a job, volunteer experience, avocation or hobby?

- Under what circumstances did you do it?

- What skills did your activity involved?

- How often did you do this task?

- Can you point to anything positive that resulted from your efforts?

Example—Transferrable Skills From Other Experience

Situation: A recruiter who works for a college hopes to get an account executive position with a public relations firm. First action verb is research.

SAMPLE CONVERSATION

Coach: Have you ever conducted research?

Career changer: I am familiar with researching issues because I worked as a volunteer with the World Wildlife Federation.

Coach: Under what circumstances did you do research?

Career changer: I was an active member of our group's Scientists' Liaison committee. I did scientific literature reviews to find scientists whose work had an impact on wildlife issues we were promoting. I would then speak to the author of the study and contact others he or she suggested to get even more information.

Coach: What skills were involved in doing this research?

Career changer: Familiarity with how reference books are organized, for one. Also, the ability to come up with key words to start the information search. My knowledge of how to search for information on the Internet and through computer databases came in handy, too.

Coach: How often did you do this kind of research?

Career changer: About ten hours every month.

Coach: Can you point to any results of your research work?
Career changer: Yes. I have already been involved in the research of four major projects. After being accepted by the committee head and the scientific consultant our organization retains, my research was used to define causes we supported and was cited in four separate campaigns, one of which was credited with being pivotal in raising $1 million to help save rain forests in Guyana.

What to Enter on the Transferable Skills Worksheet

- Researched issues as World Wildlife Federation volunteer

- Reviewed literature and interviewed scientists who did studies

- Familiarity with reference books and Internet; able to conduct key word searches manually or on computer databases

- Did ten hours of research monthly for last year

- Work accepted by committee head and scientific consultant and used in four separate campaigns—one credited with being pivotal in raising $1 million to help save rain forests in Guyana

Ready, set, start asking questions! You have fifteen minutes.

TRANSLATE TRANSFERABLE SKILLS INTO EASILY UNDERSTOOD LANGUAGE

The next step is to go over your Transferable Skills Worksheet and decide how to phrase these experiences on your revised resume. The most important thing is to use the right terminology and jargon that will be readily understood by an employer in the industry you hope to work in.

For example, if the high school teacher presented in the example on page 58 completed the exercise, her page might look like this:

EXAMPLE 1
TRANSFERABLE SKILLS WORKSHEET

Other Experience

Transferable Experience	Resume Copy
1. *Developed lesson plans*	1. *Developed course outline*
2. *Came up with interesting assignments*	2. *Designed innovative learning tasks*
3. *Published best papers in class newspaper*	3. *Well versed in using motivational tools*
4. *Involved analytical skills and teamwork, imagination, and creativity*	4. *Able to integrate needs/concerns/missions of different groups with vested interest in project outcome*
5. *Knowing what would motivate students, keep their attention, and affect their participation*	5. *Presented material to a group that was well received and elicited excellent participation*

You and your coach should go down your own list item by item and brainstorm about possibilities for better ways to phrase each in light of your new job target. A thesaurus can be helpful; so can *The Job Hunter's Word Finder* by James Bluemond (Peterson's). The bottom line: Come up with language that will make it easy for a prospective employer to see that you not only understand what the job tasks of your new career choice are, but have already done them in another context.

Before you start translating your transferable experience into resume copy, however, read through Chapter 5, Coming Up with Great Resume Language, which begins on the next page.

5 ► COMING UP WITH GREAT RESUME LANGUAGE

STEP 4
FINDING THE RIGHT WORDS

Time for this exercise: 15 minutes
Total elapsed time: 55 minutes

Your next task is to consolidate the responsibilities and accomplishments of each job into concise statements. Don't feel restricted to using the words you have on your Fact Sheets (or, if you're a career changer, on your Transferable Skills Work Sheet). It's likely that the description of the job responsibility or accomplishment will be too long. As you and your coach edit each entry, search for words that will link thoughts or more clearly convey the task.

You may want to do the same for entries on your Activities Fact Sheet, particularly if the skills you used in your activities are relevant to your new job target.

Begin each one with an action verb and use past tense (*coordinated* instead of the present tense *coordinate*) for all except your current job. Avoid making the verb a noun (i.e., instead of *negotiation skills* write *negotiate*). Don't end the verb with -ing.

Example 1
What you entered on your Work Experience Fact Sheet:
- Handled fourteen calls from customers per hour
- Was cited five times as employee of the month
- Developed good listening skills
- Learned how to ask the right questions of customers
- Studied changes in company pricing policies so I could explain them to customers
- Developed expertise in handling customers with complaints

How to translate it on your resume:

- Handled an average of fourteen customer calls per hour (four calls higher than average)

- Explained company pricing policies and solved customer complaints

- Awarded "employee of the month" recognition five times for my expertise and efficiency in helping customers

Note: You might choose some of the words from your worksheets to feature in a qualifications summary. In this example, they might be:

- Well-developed listening and interviewing skills

- Ability to handle difficult customers

- Quick study/can keep on top of changing pricing and procedures.

Example 2
What you entered on your Work Experience Fact Sheet:

- Generating new fund-raising ideas;
  Result: new annual fund-raising campaign—10 percent increase first year, about 5 percent growth last three years

- Maintaining relationships with benefactors: Writing personal letters, making phone calls, producing a newsletter, making in-person visits.

- Identifying new potential donors

- Managing a five-member staff
  Result: Improved morale, reduced turnover

How to translate it on your resume:

- Generated innovative fund-raising ideas that resulted in a 10 percent increase in contributions in 1992 and 5 percent growth each year, 1993–96

- Maintained relationships with benefactors through personal letters, phone calls, newsletter (introduced in 1993), and in-person visits

- Identified more than 1,000 new donors by developing a new computer database based on purchased lists

- Improved morale and reduced turnover among a staff of five by developing nonfinancial incentive plan that gave employees time-off credits for reaching their fund-raising goals

Even if you feel comfortable putting pen to paper, you may find the task of condensing your interview notes into the highly specific shorthand language of a resume daunting. If so, try using one of these easy-to-follow formulas:

Formula 1

(A) Action verb (present tense for a current job; past tense for a previously held job) plus

(B) Object or people plus

(C) To or for whom; of, on or from what; by, through or with what

Examples

- Promoted—pet products and accessories—at trade shows

- Designed—corporate retirement plans—for client companies

- Analyzed—effectiveness—of inventory system

Formula 2

(A) Compound action verbs plus

(B) Object quantified and/or described plus

(C) To or for whom; of, on or from what; by, through or with what plus

(D) Descriptor

Examples

- Created and implemented—database program—for direct-mail catalog operation

- Demonstrated—new customer services—to sales representatives—on a weekly basis

- Negotiated—contracts—with equipment maintenance managers—in ten foreign countries

Don't feel confined by these formulas; they are merely guidelines for getting your word across clearly and simply.

If you need ideas for action verbs, consult the chart that follows the example. It contains synonyms for ten action verbs that describe job tasks. For more help in coming up with descriptive action verbs, consult the Action Word Synonym Finder on page 66. Or get *The Job Hunter's Word Finder* by James Bluemond (Peterson's).

You should also edit your entries so that you communicate the maximum information in the minimum number of words. For example:

What you entered on your Work Experience Fact Sheet:

- In charge of nursing care unit annual report—involves tallying patient counts and turnover, selecting comments from surveys from patients and families, and written feedback from doctors and other professional personnel—(31 words)

- Make sure patients are matched to nurses most familiar with their medical condition, and monitor progress of nurse-patient teams on a daily basis to insure best possible care (28 words)

How to translate it on your resume:

- Maintain quality patient care by delegating appropriate patient-care assignments and monitoring nurse-patient relationships (14 words)

- Produce nursing care unit annual report, featuring patient information and feedback from patients, their families, doctors, and other staff professionals (20 words)

If you have not yet begun inputting any information into your computer (and you have one available), now is a good time to start. If you have already keyed in information asked for on the fact sheets, it's a good idea to do this exercise on

Action Word Synonym Finder

Calculate	Care for	Coordinate	Decide
Analyze	Administer to	Arrange	Determine
Compute	Attend to	Assign	Evaluate
Estimate	Look after	Organize	Judge
Figure	Serve	Regulate	Select
Take account of	Watch over	Systematize	Weigh

Manage	Market	Mediate	Route
Administer	Deal in	Accommodate	Direct
Head	Sell	Bring to terms	Expedite
Lead	Promote	Intercede	Guide
Oversee	Shop	Reconcile	Schedule
Supervise		Settle	Track

Train	Write
Coach	Communicate
Inform	Compile
Instruct	Compose
Teach	Draft
Tutor	

your computer keyboard (whether you're refining your resume language from handwritten notes or notes you or your coach have been keeping on the computer). It will save you the time of keying in the information you write down later on.

If your word processing program has a word-counting feature, you can get quick counts of how long your revised job descriptions and accomplishments are by keyboarding the text now. By condensing the number of words used to describe a job responsibility or accomplishment, you can streamline that entry and keep your resume easy to read and to the point. If you do not have access to a computer, use a second copy of the fact sheets to do this exercise so that you can keep each refinement you make legible and easy to follow.

You can start work now, unless you feel you could benefit by reading the following section. You have fifteen minutes.

How to Make an Ordinary Job Sound Important

Most people have, at one time or another, worked in jobs in which the responsibilities don't seem all that important, at least when they're listed on paper. You can, however, make your contributions come across more impressively by thinking about how what you did contributed to the success of the department or organization and by using descriptive language.

Consider these examples:

Job: Laborer, Sonny's Landscaping
Typical description of job responsibilities:

- Made deliveries by truck

- Unloaded shrubs, trees, and plants

- Got customer to sign delivery invoice

Enhanced description of job responsibilities:

- Transported and unloaded shrubs, plants and trees without incurring damage

- Offered tips to customers on placement and maintenance

- Explained nursery return policy, secured signature from customer

Job: Receptionist, Smith, Smith & Jackson Law Firm
Typical description of job responsibilities:

- Answered the phone

- Greeted clients

- Helped out with mailings

Enhanced description of job responsibilities:

- Mastered phone system; directed an average of 100 calls per day

- Greeted an average of ten clients daily

- Used downtime to help secretaries with mailings and to learn computer system and Microsoft Word 5.1

STEP 5
WHAT ARE YOU AN EXPERT AT?

Time for this exercise: 5 minutes
Total elapsed time: 60 minutes

At this point, you have drafted new copy for your resume. Now it's time to analyze the collection of job tasks and accomplishments so that you can identify your areas of expertise.

Why is this important? "Forcing yourself to think about your background in categories of skills, experience, and knowledge helps you mentally organize your thoughts for an interview and is particularly good preparation for answering that often-asked question, 'Tell me about yourself,' " says Richard Chagnon of Right Associates.

Beyond that, it's a way to get a sense of which items should be emphasized. You have already identified the areas of expertise required in your job target. The tasks and accomplishments that fit under those headings should be the first ones mentioned under each job entry. You may even want to edit out those that do not fit under those headings.

Finally, because you are constructing the skeleton of a functional resume in this step, you will be able to decide whether this kind of format may work better for you than a chronological one (one that lists positions held in chronological order beginning with the most recent one). The next chapter will discuss the issue of formats in greater detail.

Here's what you and your coach should do: Make a list of the action verbs and a key noun that begin each task or accomplishment on your list. Then decide under which of the three or four areas of expertise needed for your job target each belongs. (Refer back to Chapter 3, Develop a Job Target, on page 37 if necessary.)

Example 1—Recent Graduate

John is a recent graduate who majored in marketing. The following items are descriptions of job tasks he performed in a variety of sports-related, part-time, and summer jobs and in school activities.

His job target is to sell advertising space for a sports publication. The three main areas of expertise he has identified for that job target are **Communications, Market Research,** and **Sales.**

John's List of Job Responsibilities, Skills, and Involvement in Activities

Assisted sports director and weekend anchor in gathering sports information and interviewing sports personalities in Buffalo area
Communications

Supervised swimmers and enforced rules at college pool during free swim times   Does not fit any of three selected areas of expertise

Identified successful alumni business owners (potential corporate donors) through library and phone research   Market Research

Assisted in all phases of expanding readership of local sports publication; circulation increased 10 percent in six months   Sales

Persuaded previous alumni donors to increase their donations and alumni who never donated to pledge; surpassed $ 5,000 goal by $2,500   Sales

Targeted prospective advertiser for the special sales department of radio station   Market Research

Served as a parking lot attendant at sports complex   Does not fit any of three selected areas of expertise

Interviewed coaches and team players and developed sports stories for student newspaper   Communications

Sold outdoor products for home center chain; twice nominated salesperson of the month   Sales

John should highlight those items that support the three areas of expertise that his job target requires—**Communications, Market Research,** and **Sales.** In a chronological resume, that can be done by positioning those items in the first or second bullets under each job. (He may want to mention the two other items that did not fit under any of the three main categories but make them less prominent).

Example 2—Job Hunter With Experience

Patty is an operations director for a major retailer. The following list of items describes her job responsibilities and accomplishments in her present position.

Patty's next job target is to find a job as a relocation director for a major corporation with satellite divisions. Identified areas of expertise required are **Contract Negotiation, Financial Planning,** and **Communications**

Because several items on her list did not fit under any of these headings, the job hunter and coach consulted the Areas of Expertise box on page 40 and decided that **Management** and **Administration** were the appropriate headings for these items.

Plan budgets ___Financial Planning_____

Reduced expenditures ___Financial Planning_____

Present recommendations to management ___Communications____

Negotiate contracts ___Contract Negotiation_____

Supervise contractor performance ___Management_____

Manage facility openings/closings ___Management_____

Produce systems manuals ___Communications_____

Provide support services ___Administration_____

Negotiate services of subcontractors ___Contract Negotiation___

Prepare/submit bids ___Contract Negotiation_____

Supervise operations managers ___Management_____

Direct training programs ___Administration_____

On her new resume, this job hunter should emphasize the job tasks or accomplishments that were marked **Communications, Financial Planning,** or **Contract Negotiation.** In a chronological resume, that can be done by positioning those job tasks/accomplishments in the first or second bullets under each job. Why? Because the resume reader is more likely to read the first and second bullets under each job. If they're interesting, the reader will pay more attention to the ones that follow. If not, he or she may skip over them.

In a functional resume, the section headings could be the areas of expertise—in this case, **Communications, Financial Planning,** and **Contract Negotiation.**

Again, the clearer you make the connection between your skills and accomplishments and the areas of expertise in your job target, the easier it will be for an employer to recognize that you are a viable candidate.

The clock is ticking. You have five minutes!

6 ▶ THE ISSUE OF RESUME FORMAT

The chronological resume is still the preferred format and with good reason: It's the most readily understood and reader-friendly format. Jobs are arranged in a time line, starting with your current or most recent position and working back from there, ultimately listing your first job last.

People who spend much of their work days reviewing resumes—personnel agency counselors, executive recruiters, and human resources staff—are partial to a chronological format because it makes their jobs easier. They can easily identify job titles, the names of employers, and dates of employment.

When some employers see a nontraditional format, they think a candidate is either trying to cover up job changes or doesn't have career direction or much to sell, so they eliminate the candidate. Chronological resumes are also preferred by human resources people because the placement of dates next to facts makes reference checking easier.

A chronological format should probably be your choice if:

- You're looking for your first job after graduating from high school, community college, a four-year college, or graduate school

- You want to make a lateral move to a related area within your field

- You are hoping to change industries but remain in the same type of position

- You have worked for employers likely to be known to the people who will be reviewing your resume

- You are applying for a job in a traditional, conservative field such as banking, accounting, insurance, or law

- You have been working in one field or in similar job functions in related fields throughout your career and plan to look for your next position in the same or a related field

Chronological resumes, however, are not right for everyone. "They look good if your career has been linear, but if you have changed direction or experienced a job glitch, they may be seen as evidence of failure," says Richard J. Chagnon, senior vice president with Right Associates.

The best alternative is a functional resume—that is, one whose main section includes headings by areas of expertise followed by a brief work history and education section.

Some job hunters (and those who advise them) do not believe in using dates to identify when positions were held or skills used. But omitting dates is problematic: A prospective interviewer cannot tell what you did when. And in technical fields, where state-of-the-art skills are critical, recruiters and employers need to know what you have been doing most recently and how long ago you used technical skills you have listed on your resume.

Even in fields where technical skills are not critical or even considered, employers say they need to be reassured that you are not trying to disguise gaps in your employment history by using a functional resume. Suggestions for how to make a functional resume "time-conscious" are given in Chapter 7, Create a Working Draft.

You might want to consider a functional format if:

- You are a career changer who hopes to put skills learned in one profession to work in a new one (and the relationship between what you have done and what you would like to do is not obvious)

- You have worked in a variety of jobs in different fields or functional areas and need to demonstrate connections among your skills and areas of expertise

Another option is a combination chronological/functional resume. The primary advantage of a functional resume—its analysis of your strengths by areas of expertise—is added to a chronological resume, often as a second page. Why use this format? It's a way to emphasize groups of skills or experience that can help the resume reader more readily see why you are qualified for a position.

Most resume books include what is called an analytical or targeted format. It presents what you know and what you have done as individual skills and achievements grouped under headings such as "Capabilities" and "Accomplishments."

This type of resume is not presented in this book because most employers don't know what to make of it. And if an employer is having a difficult time getting a handle on you as a candidate, he or she is likely to put your resume aside (and perhaps never get back to reviewing it further) or reject it out of hand.

Another problem: An analytical resume does not lend itself as easily to identifying when you used your skills or accomplished results listed. The most often cited reason for opting for this resume format—defining your experiences so that they fit a specific position you hope to get—can be done more easily and just as effectively in one of the other three formats. You can find examples of all three types in Chapter 12, 90-Minute Results.

INFORMATION SEQUENCE WITHIN FORMATS

Here's the order in which you should list sections of information for the chronological format:

- Identification (name, address, phone number)
- Job Objective or Summary of Qualifications (both optional)
- Work Experience
- Activities or Professional Involvement/Affiliations
- Skills (optional)
- Education
- Interests

The exception to this sequence guideline is the recent graduate or experienced job hunter who is working on or has recently completed an academic program that is a prerequisite for moving into a new functional area, job level, or industry. If that's your situation, you may want to highlight that experience by putting your Education section before your Work Experience section. It's a judgment call that varies with each situation; if you feel your work experience is more important, feature it first and follow it with your Education section.

In a functional format, the sequence would be the following:

- Identification
- Job Objective or Summary of Qualifications (both optional)
- Areas of Expertise
- Work History
- Skills (optional)
- Education
- Interests

For a combination chronological/functional resume, use the chronological sequence and start your second page with an Identification section followed by an Areas of Expertise section.

If you are unsure which format is best for you, talk it over with your coach before you begin the next step.

7 ▶ CREATE A WORKING DRAFT

STEP 6

BUILD A RESUME THAT WORKS

Time for this exercise: 25 minutes
Total elapsed time: 85 minutes

Now you're at the top of the stretch. The next step—combining your notes and the marked up copy of your resume into a legible working draft—will be gratifying because you will see the results of the previous hour's efforts.

If you have access to a computer, that's best; a typewriter is a good second choice. Whoever is the most proficient keyboarder—you or your coach—should input the copy. Although you can create a resume in your word processing program, you can also type it in using the template that is featured on the disk that comes with this book. The person who is not keyboarding should play the role of editor and look for any errors or make final editing suggestions.

If neither a computer nor typewriter is available, neatly transfer the copy onto one sheet so that it will be easy to read. If you're revising a resume, you may be able to cut and paste sections from an untouched copy of your current resume and mark revisions by hand.

Here's a section-by-section guide on what should be included in each section. Read each one before you keyboard or print your copy for that section.

Identification

- Your full name (a formal name rather than a nickname is preferable).

- Your permanent address—street number and name, apartment number, city, state, and zip code. If you are relocating, it's a good idea to give a local address. If you will only be at that address temporarily, you may also want to include a second address at which you can receive mail beyond a time you indicate.

Example

(Temporary Address—4/96–6/96)	(Permanent Address)
Marriott Residence Inn	6263 Forrest Drive
777 Cypriot Way	Tenafly, NJ 04736
Palo Alto, CA 97801	

- Contact information. Include a phone number where you (or someone who can take a message for you) can be reached during working hours. If that is problematic for any reason, consider investing in an answering machine, telephone answering service, or voice messaging service offered by your local phone company. List your work number if you can comfortably accept a phone call from a prospective employer. If you check your e-mail regularly, it doesn't hurt to include your e-mail address; more and more people in a growing number of fields use e-mail as regularly as they do the telephone. A scanning tip: List each phone number (and your e-mail address) on its own line.

If you are revising a resume and have included any other personal information—social security number, birth date, marital status, number of dependents, health status, height, or weight—delete it. These details are unnecessary and some may cause you to be ruled out as a candidate because they may play into an employer's prejudices. He may feel that he would ideally like a single person who is free to put in extra hours after work or on weekends, or, conversely, that a married candidate is a better bet because he or she is more "stable."

The Job Objective

Even though you have a written job target, which was used to help you develop the content of your resume, it may not be necessary or advisable to include it on the resume itself. Before you decide whether it makes sense in your case, consider these pros and cons:

PRO: A job objective, even a general one, is useful when sending your resume to an employer who is simultaneously receiving resumes for more than one type of position. In short: A job objective is a shorthand way of routing resumes to the right person or pile. That's almost always the case with personnel departments and departments or divisions of large firms.

CON: A job objective that states the obvious is unnecessary and takes up space. If your career follows a progression well understood in your industry, it makes more sense to talk about why you are interested in a particular job or company in your cover letter.

PRO: A job objective can be useful to the resume reviewer if you hope to do anything out of the ordinary, in particular, switching job functions, industries, or fields. What you choose to emphasize about your experience, of course, should support your candidacy.

CON: A specific objective may narrow your options. If your objective states that you are looking for a position as a paralegal with a litigation department, you may take yourself out of the running if the firm you have applied to has just disbanded its litigation department or its only current opening is for a paralegal in its corporate department. That would not be a problem, of course, if you were ONLY willing to consider a job involving litigation work. One way to solve the problem is to have more than one resume, each of which features its own unique job objective and emphasizes skills or experiences that support that objective.

If you decide to include a job objective on your resume, keep the following in mind:

- Speak not of what your employer can do for you but what you can do for an employer.

  ### Example: Self-serving job objective

  —A creative position in which I can fully utilize my artistic and design skills and gain more direct client experience

  ### Employer-focused job objective

  —A position in a graphic arts department that would allow me to contribute my artistic and design experience to projects that would enhance the firm's relationships with clients

- Be careful in your use of self-attributed qualities.

  ### Example: Self-congratulatory wording

  —A challenging position that would put to good use my excellent public speaking and considerable fund-raising skills

  ### Better use of self-attributed strengths

  —A senior development position that requires extensive public speaking experience and a track record of successful fund-raising efforts

- Avoid overused adjectives and phrases that provide no useful information.

  ### Example

  —A creative, self-motivated professional seeks the opportunity to grow within a progressive organization

- Do not talk about your long-term goals. Mentioning them can be counterproductive, particularly if you say that you would eventually like to be the boss or start your own business.

Summary of Qualifications

Some people feel that adding a key word section at the top of a r resume maximizes a computer's ability to ready your resume and get "hits" (a hit is when one of your skills matches the requirement of the employer doing the search). But so long as you use key words that describe your skills, experience, and work attributes throughout your resume, say the makers of electronic resume-processing systems, you won't gain anything from creating a discrete key word section at the top. To help human readers of your resume, however, you may want to add a summary section so that they can get an at-a-glance sense of whether to spend more than the average minute or two reading your resume.

Making general statements about your work habits and personality qualities isn't very helpful:

Example

Strong communications skills. Proficient in organizational skills and attention to detail. Able to anticipate problems before they arise. Self-motivated, able to work under pressure.

A short, fact-filled summary with statements or examples that back up claims about your abilities, on the other hand, can be effective:

Example 1—Recent graduate

Four summers of experience working as a reservations agent for a major hotel chain • Bachelor's degree in hotel and restaurant management • Fluent in Spanish and French • In the words of my supervisor: "Works comfortably with the sophisticated business client and the leisure travel client; maintains a sense of humor under pressure."

Example 2—Job hunter with experience

Five years of experience as a legal editor/proofreader, editing briefs for U.S. Federal Court cases. A master's degree in English and one year of law school have helped me hone my ability to catch errors of grammar, content and format. Partners feel comfortable signing off on my work with minimal review. Proficient Word 5.1 user who, in the words of my boss, "Maintains a sense of humor even under the worst deadline pressure."

Example 3—Job hunter with experience interested in changing industries

A senior human resource manager who has worked for three Fortune 500 firms during the last fifteen years, developing expertise in:

Employee relations • Recruiting and selection • Personnel administration • Health plan administration • Employee training and development • Wage and salary Administration • Outplacement

CREATE YOUR WORK EXPERIENCE SECTION

Work Experience is one of the most popular headings for this section. Other options include Employment, Business History, Work History, Experience, Employment Experience, Professional Experience, or Professional Background. If you are a recent graduate who has work experience related to your job target, you might want to create two work sections: Professional Experience and Other Work Experience (or Summer and Part-time Jobs).

The following information should be part of each job subheading:

- Job title

- Company name

- Dates of employment

Including the company location (city, state) is a good idea if you have worked in a geographic location different from the one where you're now job hunting. It's not necessary to include:

- Headings that state the categories (i.e., Job title, Dates of employment, Name of employer)

- The address or phone number of the employer or the name and job title of your manager (they can be included on a separate reference sheet)

If your job titles reflect the fact that you have steadily advanced in your career or that you have worked in a number of related jobs in the field you have targeted, make them the most prominent piece of information:

Example

Technical Writer, Information Services, Inc., Wellesley, Massachusetts, 6/95 to present

If your job titles do not tell as impressive a story as the names of your employers, position company names first.

Example

Andersen Consulting, Palo Alto, California
Office Administrator, 1991–present

Placing dates of employment flush left (instead of having them follow the name or location of the employer) and indenting the other components is a good choice if you want to emphasize your work continuity:

Example

1/94–present	Publicity Associate, Hilton Hotels International, Chicago, Illinois
5/91–12/93	Front Desk Clerk, Hilton Hotels International, New York, New York

If you have worked in several positions at one company, it's best to mention the company name and location first, then list the job title and dates you worked in that position:

Example

Jones, Jones & Smith Law Offices, Houston, Texas, 1989–present
Office Administrator, 1994–present
Bookkeeper, 1991–1993
Receptionist, 1989–1991

If the company or companies you worked for are small and/or not likely to be known to the people reviewing your resume, it's a smart idea to add a short description of the company after its name. Another way to handle this is to work the company description into the sentence describing your responsibilities and accomplishments.

Example 1—Recent graduate

Customer Service Representative, Child's Play (a mail-order catalog featuring educational toys), Denver, Colorado, November 1995 to present

Example 2—Job hunter with experience

Senior Tax Adviser, Crawley Communications, Inc. (a large regional cable television company), Denver, Colorado, November 1988 to present

The next section is for those who are planning to use a functional format. If that's not you, page ahead to "Four Steps to Tighter Copy" on page 82.

HOW TO PRESENT WORK EXPERIENCE IN A FUNCTIONAL FORMAT

You have already identified the main areas of expertise of your new job target in Step 5: What Are You an Expert At on page 68. Now you need to select the descriptions of tasks or accomplishments from each job you have held and put them under the appropriate heading. Each entry should begin with an action verb. It's best to use past tense with all action verbs, except for descriptions of current job tasks. List the year or years you performed or accomplished each after each entry (see the following example). Eliminate job descriptions or accomplishments that do not relate to the kind of position you hope to land.

Example 1

Situation: Kim Pressler has held administrative and teaching jobs at one college since receiving her master's degree from the institution in 1988. Her new job target is a position in event coordination with a corporation or meeting-planning organization. Her current resume, which uses a chronological format, has the following work experience section:

Work Experience
Michigan State University, East Lansing, Michigan, 1988–present

College Adviser, 1994–present
      —Help 150 freshmen plan their curricula
      —Initiated tutoring program for students on academic probation
      —Coordinate ten major freshman events, including Freshman Family Day, Opening Day activities, and Freshman Orientation

Program Assistant, Arts and Sciences Division, 1993–94
      —Organized faculty committee to review goals and objectives of core curriculum
      —Conducted curriculum update workshops for faculty advisers
      —Wrote new course catalog for students studying abroad

Instructor, English Department, 1991–92
      —Developed and taught remedial writing course, which received faculty recognition at an honors banquet
      —Supervised three teaching assistants who graded freshman compositions

Faculty Adviser, Student Activities Office, 1988–1990
      —Reviewed decisions of elected student officers on bookings of entertainment and cultural events for campus
      —Monitored expenditures of $800,000 of student activity fee budget

Kim realized that she had experience in four skill areas—communications, event coordination, management, and planning—that related to her next career goal. She rearranged the descriptions under her jobs to fit the appropriate categories.

After identifying the areas of expertise of her new job target, she grouped her job tasks and accomplishments under the appropriate headings—Event

Coordination, Planning, Communications, and Management. She arranged the categories in order of descending importance and added accomplishments and numbers to support her role in the two top categories, Event Coordination and Planning. Thus, her revised Work Experience section reads as follows:

Event Coordination
—Coordinated ten major freshman events involving 1,000 students and a support team of 100 staff and administrators; participation rate jumped to 90–100 percent, exceeding earlier rates of 70–95 percent, 1994–present
—Organized faculty committee to review goals and objectives of core curriculum; the proposals of the committee were unanimously adopted by the president and board of trustees; subsequently asked by several deans to organize such committees for their disciplines, 1993–94

Planning
—Helped 150 freshmen plan their curricula; by working 60-hour weeks over two weeks succeeded in resolving 50 scheduling problems, 1994–present
—Initiated tutoring program for students on academic probation; 75 participate each semester, 95 percent of whom go off probation, 1994–present

Communications
—Wrote new course catalog for students studying abroad, 1993–94
—Developed and taught remedial writing course, which received faculty recognition at an honors banquet, 1992–93
—Conduct curriculum update workshops for faculty advisers, 1993–94

Management
—Supervised three teaching assistants who graded freshman compositions, 1990–92
—Reviewed decisions of elected student officers on bookings of entertainment and cultural events on campus, 1988–89
—Monitored expenditures of $500,000 of student activity fee money, 1988–89

If, through your activities, you have developed skills that support your new job target, it's acceptable and advisable to list each under the appropriate area of expertise. it's a good idea to mention the context in which you acquired the skill or got the result.

Example 2

Situation: A job hunter has worked as a volunteer, assisting her pastor in visiting families whose loved one was dying. She hopes to find a paid position as a hospice counselor with a community organization or hospital. In a functional resume, this job hunter's volunteer experience could be listed under the heading of Counseling:

Counseling

Served as a volunteer grief counselor to children and their families, 1993–present

—Listened to and consoled those who had experienced a loss

—Offered help in making funeral and memorial arrangements

—Made suggestions about community agencies that could assist family with financial, insurance, and legal matters

Now, create a job history section. List your job title, the name of the employer, location if necessary (city and state only), and the dates of employment. For additional ideas on how this information could be presented, read the section following the example.

Example

Indiana University, Bloomington, Indiana, 1994–present

College Adviser, 1994–present

Program Assistant, Arts and Sciences Division, 1993–94

Instructor, English Department, 1990–92

Faculty Adviser, Student Activities Office, 1988–89

Four Steps to Tighter Copy

To get the maximum information in the minimum space, carefully edit your entries under each job.

1. Look for repetition. It's most likely to occur in your description of job tasks. Decide where it's most appropriate and delete the second reference.

   If, for example, you were a flight attendant and were later promoted to flight service manager, a job task that would be applicable to both is:

   —Ensure strong customer relations through good service

   Because you are likely to mention more sophisticated tasks in the higher-level job, you can assume that customer service will be implicit in one or more of these descriptions. That's the case in the following example:

   —Advise or mediate any passenger problems beyond the experience or control of the crew

2. Tighten up your draft by eliminating unnecessary words. All of the following are unnecessary:

- Responsible for
- Know how to do
- Involved in
- Worked as a (job title)
- Experienced in
- Conversant in (or with)

3. Incorporate accomplishments as clauses in your description of your job tasks. For example:

—Explained membership benefits to potential health-club clients, efforts that resulted in fifty new members in ten months

4. Eliminate jobs that are "ancient history." If you are an experienced job hunter, preprofessional, summer, and part-time jobs you had during school should be the first to go. Once a job or group of jobs is no longer relevant to your career, you can dispense with them in a line or two. If you can include an accomplishment or two, do. For instance:

—1980–1985 Rose to level of department manager after working in several J.C. Penney stores as a retail salesperson. Was recognized as "Department Manager of the Month" five times in two years, a store record.

CREATE YOUR EDUCATION SECTION

Start with the last school you attended or graduated from and list each entry in reverse chronological order. It's not necessary to include every school you ever attended. Each entry should start with either the name of your degree or the name of the college. The further away you get from your college experience, the more selective you should be about what you include. Information you should list in your Education section includes:

- Type of degree received (B.A., B.S., M.B.A., M.A., M.S., and Ph.D. are all easily recognized degrees and need not be spelled out; any others should be unless you are certain the initials will be recognized by people in the field in which you are job hunting).

- The name of your university. Do not use an acronym (for example, OSU for Ohio State University). If the location is not obvious from the name or its reputation, provide the city and state.

- The year you received your degree.

- Your major field of study and any significant honors (i.e., graduating with distinction or Phi Beta Kappa). It's not necessary to include your grade point average (however spectacular) once you have your first, full-time job experience on your resume.

Example

M.S.W., Ohio State University, 1995,
$500 Top Departmental Thesis Award

- How much of your education you personally financed through scholarships or part-time or summer jobs (it can be expressed as a percentage). A statement of this kind shows that you are a highly motivated person and that you can successfully juggle more than one commitment at a time—both highly prized qualities in today's workplace. Consider deleting this information once you have been out of school five to seven years.

Example

> B.A., Political Science, George Washington University, 1996
> Financed 50 percent of educational expenses through part-time and summer jobs

Listing courses is usually not necessary; the exception is if they were skill specific and likely to be important to prospective employers.

If you have completed a program for which you have received a certificate or degree *after* you graduated from college or high school, that information should appear before your college (or high school) information. You can emphasize the importance of a program or explain the significance of a certificate if you add numbers or a short description.

Example

> Certificate in Electronics and Computer Technology, 1996
> (full-time two-year program) Merritt College, Oakland, CA

- Special programs of study. If you are a recent graduate and spent a summer or semester studying or working in another country or in a special program, describe it briefly after you mention the name of the school and program. Be sure to mention if your grades or another criterion were part of your being selected for participation in the program.

Example

> Summer, 1994, Hebrew University, Jerusalem, Israel Studied Hebrew and biblical literature and spent one month living and working on a kibbutz

CREATE YOUR SKILLS SECTION

In previous editions of this book, this section was listed as an optional one. In this revised edition, I strongly suggest that you include such a section on your resume because prospective employers are more likely to want to interview you if they know you can perform job tasks they need done. There are several heading options beyond simply saying Skills, which include: Technical Skills or naming your area of skill expertise—for example, Video Production Skills.

All you need to do is to set up the information you have already entered on your Skills Fact Sheet. If you're inputting information into your computer at this time, here are several examples of how you can set up your entries in this section.

Example 1–Recent graduate

Skills

—Desktop publishing, in particular Quark Xpress (mastery/used for four years, most recently in 1996) and Adobe Illustrator (mastery/used for five years, most recently in 1996)

—Stat camera operation (competent/used for two years,, most recently in 1995)

—Manual pasteup and layout methods (competent/used for three years, most recently in 1995)

Example 2—Job hunter with experience (exercise floor staff supervisor)

Skills

—Ability to spot a client who is lifting weights

—Ability to talk about abstract concepts—for example, how a muscle should feel as it is moved a certain way

—An eye for judging correct exercise form

—Ability to solve fitness/workout problems

—Working knowledge of a wide variety of fitness equipment (can explain how to use properly and for what desired result)

If you list software programs, be sure to include the version that you work on (it's usually expressed as a number, for example, Windows 95). And be sure to get the spelling and capitalization of the words right; product names often defy the rules.

CREATE YOUR ACTIVITIES SECTION

Including professional activities is always a good idea; it shows that you are interested in your field beyond what's called for in your job. If your community or volunteer involvements are significant or provide additional evidence of skills you use as a professional, they're also worth including. How many you choose to include and the detail you provide is a judgment call. The activities section may be as long as your work experience section if you're a recent graduate who has been very active in campus organizations, for example, or if as a stay-at-home parent, you've devoted a lot of time and effort to community, school, or volunteer activities.

Decide first which heading is most appropriate, given the kind of information you are presenting. Possibilities include:

- Extracurricular activities

- Professional activities or memberships

- Community or civic activities

- volunteer work

One of the best ways to give a capsule view of your activities is to list the type of affiliation you have (member, officer, committee chair), the name of the organization (and, if necessary, a brief explanation of what it is), and the dates of your involvement:

Example 1—Recent graduate

—Secretary, Undergraduate Speech Communication Association, 1994–95

—Captain, Men's Soccer Team, University of Oklahoma, 1995–96 season

Example 2—Job hunter with experience

—Local chapter president, Amherst College Alumni Association

—Member, public relations committee, Menlo Park Historical Society

Describe your accomplishments or the skills you developed if you feel they will provide further evidence of your qualifications for the job you hope to get:

Example 1—Job hunter with experience
A certified public accountant who is hoping to get a position as vice president of taxes at a corporation should include this in a Professional Involvement section:

Tax Executives Institute

—Member since 1987

—Elected president for 1994–1995 term

—Initiated new semiannual meeting focusing on new technology in the field, which drew highest level of participation in organization's history

Example 2—Career changer

An account executive for a public relations firm who hopes to find a position as a press liaison for a lobbying organization would want to include the following:

Campaign Coordinator, City Council Member, East Lansing, Michigan 1995

—Coordinated successful campaign of first-time city council member in a race the press described as a "shoo-in" for the incumbent

—Orchestrated twenty events at which my candidate spoke

—Handled more than 100 inquiries and interviews with the local press

If you have been out of school for three or more years and still have college activities listed on your resume, you can probably eliminate them. If you have been working for three years or less and participated in activities in college that you feel support your career interest and involvement, keep the list short and sweet. Mention the name of the organization, the role you played and briefly describe your responsibilities, or, better yet, an accomplishment or two. For example, a high school physical education teacher/coach who hopes to find a job working as a G.O. (initials for the French words, *gentil organisateur*, or "congenial organizer" in English) at a Club Med might include the following in his Activities section:

University of California, Santa Cruz, Crew Team 8/91–5/93
—1993 West Coast Champions

A public relations associate at a PR agency who hopes to find a similar job in a Fortune 1000 company could write:

Media and Publicity Coordinator, Business Roundtable, 1995–96
—Efforts resulted in 25 mentions in student and local media

If any of your activities directly support your job target, consider putting them under an "Experience" heading that defines the area of expertise; for example, "Communications Experience," or "Counseling Experience." The fact that the experience was an internship or volunteer activity does not matter; what's more important is to emphasize to the employer that you have accumulated experience in your job target area.

For instance, a recent college graduate with a B.A. in English who hopes to land a position as a reservations agent with a tour operator might include the following activity in a section entitled "Travel and Tourism Experience":

Trip Organizer, Student Activities Organization, Michigan State University, 1995–96
—Organized and supervised a spring-break tour to Fort Lauderdale
—Collected 150 reservations and deposits

—Made hotel room assignments and performed room inspections

—Provided entertainment during 10-hour bus trip

—Net profit to Student Activities was $3,500

CREATE YOUR PREFERENCES SECTION

Since your resume may be scanned by an automated applicant-tracking system or downloaded from an on-line database, it's a good idea to let prospective employers know several things:

- The kind of work you're available for (full-time, part-time, temporary, permanent, contract)

- Geographic preferences (city and state or simply "willing to relocate")

For example, a job hunter seeking a long-term position in the U.S. Southeast might specify on his resume:

Preferences   Full-time, permanent position; Atlanta or Southeast

CREATE YOUR INTERESTS SECTION

Some people question whether to include this line or two of information that is not related to their work lives. But employers, recruiters, and outplacement people I have consulted vote "Yes." Why? Because your Interests section is the one place to give the reader of your resume an insight into who you are beyond your work identity.

Beyond that, it's a help to the interviewer because it provides an easy way to start the interview conversation. And it may turn out that the employer shares one of your passions, which can only help you as a candidate. If you have an unusual interest, for example, playing the fiddle in a Celtic music group or competing in hot-air balloon races, it may capture the fancy of the resume reader who will want to learn more about you.

A simple list of interests, even if it consists of only two items, is fine. But it's important to be specific. Saying that you enjoy fashion, films, sports, or traveling is not very revealing; it's far better to say:

- Collecting vintage clothing

- Attending major film festivals

- Coaching AYSO soccer

- Taking train trips

Another way to define your interests is to put a few words of explanation after each interest. For example:

- Karate (have earned a black belt)

- Playing the piano (have been playing a regular one-night engagement each weekend for five years)

- Black and white photography (develop and print own photos)

CREATE YOUR REFERENCES SHEET

Instead of saying "References Available on Request" at the bottom of your resume, it's a good idea to prepare a list of references on a separate sheet so that you can give it to a prospective employer at the interview.

At the top of the sheet, use the same identification heading as you did for your resume. Then center the heading "List of References." Include the following information for each reference you list: the person's name, his or her job title and phone number, and the name and address of the company. If the reference is no longer at the company where you once worked, it's a good idea to add one more line that includes the name of the company you both used to work for and your dates of employment. For example:

List of References
Max Humboldt, Vice President, Marketing
Universal Manufacturing Company
111 Oak Knoll Drive
Durham, North Carolina
919-555-8000
(SFS Manufacturing, 1991–94)

If you're a recent graduate, don't include the names of professors unless the faculty member is familiar with your working habits because of his or her advisory role to a campus organization or activity in which you were involved.

8 ▶ WHY YOU SHOULDN'T TELL WHITE LIES

You may be tempted to inflate your job title, fudge dates of employment, or exaggerate your educational credentials so that you come across as a more qualified job candidate. It's not a good idea.

Altering the truth can get you into trouble. At a minimum, most employers check out basic information: dates of employment, job title, and salary; dates of attendance and degrees received from an educational institution. If prospective employers discover inconsistencies, they are likely to take you out of consideration immediately. Their reasoning is that if you misrepresent something about yourself, how can you be trusted as an employee? If the discovery is made after you've been hired, you stand to lose your job. Even if the white lie doesn't become known immediately, you always run the risk of it being discovered later and being a source of embarrassment and perhaps worse. At the very least, you don't want to jeopardize your reputation even years from now by having someone accuse you of playing fast and loose with the truth on your resume.

In what is probably one of the most publicized cases of resume scrutiny in recent memory, the Brown & Williamson Tobacco Corp. hired a private investigation team to examine past resumes (and other documents) of a high-ranking company whistle-blower, Jeffrey Wigand. In a 500-page dossier that Brown & Williamson gave to the *Wall Street Journal* (in an effort to discredit Wigand's integrity), the company included a list entitled "Lies on Wigand's Resume." The *Wall Street Journal* story said, "And B&W identified several cases of incorrect dates and some exaggerated claims in his resume and the outplacement interview, misstatements that Mr. Wigand now concedes."

The bottom line is that the edge you think you gain by telling a white lie isn't worth the risk. Be sure to avoid committing telling any of the following:

Disguising work gaps. However tempting it is to make your work history look continuous, don't extend the period you actually worked for an employer to cover up the time you spent job hunting, even if it was months. It only takes one phone call from a prospective employer to verify your time with a company; an inconsistency can only work against you. Suggestions for what to say about this specific situation will be covered in "Secrets of a Successful Cover Letter" on page 108.

Of course, you should be prepared to explain a work gap in an interview. Caring for a seriously ill relative, managing a family business or affairs after the death of a parent or sibling, or recovering from an accident or illness yourself are increasingly understood as reasonable explanations for work gaps.

If you have taken time out from your career to raise a family, a line of explanation at the appropriate chronological point is one option. For example:

1990–present—Left full-time employment to raise two young children.

If a period of unemployment occurred one or more jobs ago, chances are the gap will not be used to screen you out. Most hiring managers would assume that the employer or employers who hired you after you were unemployed checked out the gap and did not consider it a problem, so they wouldn't either.

If you do not want to call attention to a period of unemployment that was in the past, using years rather than months and years is acceptable. Omitting dates altogether is a mistake because each reader of your resume will assume something that may not be true—that you have an addiction or health problem, that you leave a job anytime you are offered more money elsewhere, that you are older than you really are. The outcome: You won't get a call for an interview.

Changing job titles. The risk of inflating your job title to make your job or responsibilities sound more important than they really are (or were) is that it's easy to get caught. Job titles are one of the few things that personnel departments routinely provide to prospective employers who inquire.

If, however, your job title does not accurately reflect the scope and importance of your responsibilities, you can change it to make it more accurately reflect what you do. "Many job titles are confusing at best and misleading at worst," says John D. Erdlen of Strategic Outsourcing, Inc. To avoid the possibility of any misunderstanding, however, he suggests that you clarify what you did in an interview situation; that is, mentioning that your actual job title was "X" but that you took the liberty of changing the wording on your resume to make clearer what you did.

Inventing academic credentials. It's downright dangerous to claim you attended or graduated from a particular school or college if you didn't. Just as bad is awarding yourself a degree you never earned. If a position you want to apply for requires a certain educational background, be honest about your credentials and explain in your cover letter why you should nonetheless be considered.

Exaggerating your capabilities. Being self-confident is a plus, but overstating your knowledge or expertise on paper may be cause for embarrassment. You may be asked a technical question in an interview that you are unable to answer and be ruled out as a candidate as a result. Even if your lack of know-how doesn't surface in an interview and you're hired, you may be setting yourself up for failure if you are subsequently given responsibilities that you cannot handle.

Taking more credit than you deserve. It's fine to describe your contributions to a successful project, but saying that you initiated, supervised, or were solely responsible for something when that was not really the case is foolish. It's too easy for a prospective employer to discover what your real role was through a conversation with your former boss, colleagues, or people you both know. At the very least, your credibility will suffer, and in the worst-case scenario, you won't get an offer from the employer.

Claiming a fictitious award or recognition. Why not say that you won the divisional title as a singles player on your college tennis team (when it was really a regional award)? Or that you were elected an officer of the Rotary Club in the city you've relocated from (when you were actually a committee head who volunteered to chair the committee)? Are prospective employers really going to check? Maybe not. But maybe they will. Or the discrepancy may come to light through a connection that's hard to imagine. When it does, your credibility will suffer. And so will your chances of getting an offer.

Saying you were a freelancer or consultant. You should claim such status only if you were really engaged in such efforts; otherwise you won't have legitimate answers about questions an employer is likely to ask about your "business."

How Long Should Your Resume Be?

In previous editions of this book, I recommended that resume writers try to get everything down to a page, unless they were professors, psychologists, doctors, or in other professions where a resume of several pages was the norm. I still think that a page (or, for job hunters with a lot of experience, two pages) is advisable if you know you are going to hand your resume to a person who will be reading it. But if you're responding to a help-wanted ad or an on-line job posting, it's fine to have a resume that's several pages in length.

"Unlike human managers who may have to get through a stack of resumes within a certain time period, software programs don't get fatigued as they look for language that meets certain job criteria," explains Joseph Hnilo, vice president of Resumix, a company that licenses human resources software. In fact, says Hnilo, providing a more elaborate explanation of your background and skills can actually help your chances of being screened in.

9 ▶ PERFECT YOUR COPY

STEP 7
A FINAL LOOK: POLISHING YOUR COPY

Time for this exercise: 5 minutes
Total elapsed time: 90 minutes

The final step before you design your resume is to make sure that your copy is in its best final form. You and your coach should go down the following checklist together to look for omissions, repetitions, misspellings, and typographical errors. If you're unsure about the rationale or options for any of the items mentioned on the checklist, go back to Chapter 7, Create a Working Draft, which begins on page 74. Mark changes as you go.

Computer Time-Saver: Use your word processing program's spell-checking feature to spot typographical and spelling errors (but double check with a sight check, too).

RESUME COPY CHECKLIST

Directions: Put a check mark next to each item that should be deleted or that requires further work. You can print this form out by using the disk that comes with this book.

Identification Information

What's needed:

____ Your full name

____ Address (temporary and permanent with dates)

____ Daytime phone number

What isn't needed:

____ Social Security number

____ Work availability

____ Height, weight, or other physical characteristics

____ Number of dependents

____ Number of dependents

____ Marital status

____ Health status

____ Date of birth

Job Objective (optional)

What's needed:

____ Short (no more than two lines), clear, specific language

Summary of Qualifications (optional)

What's needed:

____ Precise skills or areas of expertise (use nouns)

____ Previous job titles/functional areas or departments in which you've worked

Section Headings

What's needed:

____ Correct sequence

____ Consistency in placement, type, and graphic treatment

Work Experience

What's needed:

____ Clauses, not complete sentences

____ Present job responsibilities in current verb tense (except in functional format—past okay for all)

____ Past job responsibilities in past verb tense

____ Acronyms or abbreviations spelled out (unless industry-related and you're sure they will be understood)

____ Different action verbs if any appear more than once

What's not needed:

____ Employer phone number

____ Name of supervisor

____ The phrase "responsible for" or "duties included"

____ The headings "position," "job title," or "duties"

____ Capitalizing words unnecessarily

____ Redundant job tasks

____ Any reference to salary

____ Reasons for leaving past job(s)

Description of Accomplishments

What's needed:

____ Job, time frame, or context in which each occurred

____ Numbers to quantify

____ Better description of results

____ More specifics

____ More examples

What's not needed:

____ Self-congratulatory wording

If using a functional format:

What's needed:

____ Three or four areas of expertise as main section headings

____ Three or four entries under each heading, each of which belongs under that heading

Education

What's needed:

____ Name of certificate/degree received and year/month awarded

____ Name of school (location—city, state if not apparent from name)

____ Major field of study (optional)

If graduation from college was within the last five years:

____ Major scholarships/awards received

____ Honors received (optional)

____ Percentage of college expenses earned through summer or part-time jobs

What's not needed:

____ Course work (unless recent and relevant to position for which you are applying)

Activities (optional)

What's needed:

____ Name of organization (several-word explanation if necessary)

_____ Brief description of role you played
_____ Dates of involvement
_____ Accomplishments (with numbers to quantify)

What's not needed:
_____ Activities not recent or relevant to job target

Skills (optional)
_____ Name of skill and one- or two-word description of skill level
_____ Versions and correctly spelled names of software programs, hardware, equipment, or processes
_____ Date when you last used the skill
_____ Context in which you used the skill (optional)

Interests
What's needed:
_____ Brief descriptions of specific activity, including any awards or recognition you received

Once you finish implementing the changes that you noted on your checklist, your 90 minutes will be up, and your content should be in excellent shape. Now it's time to create a paper version.

10 ▸ DESIGN YOUR RESUME

C ontent is king in a resume, but if there's a chance that it will be reviewed by human eyes, it's worth your while to invest the time to make it look inviting. Making your resume a visual success is something you can do yourself if you have access to a computer and know how to use a word processing program. The templates that are featured on the disk that comes with this book can simplify your task considerably.

If you're still in college, you may be able to use computers in your school's career planning and placement office. If that's not an option and you don't have access to a computer, you can rent one by the hour; the going rate is $8 to $20. Some copy shops will design your resume from handwritten or typewritten copy. If you have your copy input on a disk, all the much better; you reduce the chance of typographical errors that are the designer's fault and you may pay less since inputting copy is time-consuming. The average cost of this service varies by area of the country, but it ranges from $30 to $90 for a one-page resume and $40 to $110 for a two-page resume. Some copy shops will also make a duplicate of your resume on disk (a minor additional cost) so that you can have it updated whenever necessary. (Be sure to ask what word processing or desktop publishing program—and which version—was used to create the resume document.)

If having someone else design your resume is your choice, you can skip ahead to Chapter 11, Put Your Resume to Work, which starts on page 102.

A PRIMER ON DESIGN

You do not need to be a graphic designer to design a terrific-looking resume. If you know little or nothing about design, however, you may inadvertently make novice mistakes, such as using more than one typeface. Simplicity and readability are the most important things to keep in mind. Here is how to create a great-looking resume in six steps:

1. Select the right typeface and point size. You may be limited in your choice of typeface or font by what is available on the software program you are using.

But if you are using a fairly recent version of a popular program such as Microsoft Word or WordPerfect, you will have plenty of choices.

You can choose a serif font—one that features short cross-lines at the ends of the main strokes of the letters—or a san serif font.

Example: Serif font—M d;   Sans serif font—M d

The following list of typefaces are highly recommended for resumes. All are typefaces that can be easily read by optical scanners. The names may differ slightly (i.e., Times, Times Roman, or Times New Roman) depending on which company produced the type for the software program. The look varies slightly (but will go unnoticed by the inexperienced eye).

Serif Fonts

Times (a condensed typeface that's a good choice if you need to get a lot of text on the page)

New Century Schoolbook (a wide typeface that's a good choice if you want your text to expand to fill out a page)

Palatino (a typeface that's more distinctive than its close relative, Times)

Bookman (a wide typeface that's a good choice if you want your text to expand to fill out a page)

Sans Serif Fonts

Helvetica and Helvetica Narrow (for Macs)—a legible, clean typeface with a simple design; Helvetica Narrow allows you to get more text on the page

Optima (a thick and thin typeface that's distinctive and not as widely used as other typefaces mentioned here)

Universe and Ariel (for IBM PCs and compatibles)—the equivalent of Helvetica and Helvetica Narrow

Avoid using a script font because it is too hard to read.

Example: *It's best to avoid a script font.*

The point size—the specification for the size of the type—should be a ten to fourteen point size for the body of your resume, depending on the font. You might start by trying a ten point if you think you will have trouble getting everything on one page.

Headings should be a consistent point size; a 14-point size would make sense if you were using 12-point text; use a 12-point size for headings if you are using 10-point text. Avoid the temptation to blow up your name to a huge point size or it will look disproportionate. An 18-point size is the largest you should go if you are using 14-point headings; a 14-point size is fine is you are using 12-point headings. Subheadings (job title, employer, degree earned, college attended) should be the same point size as the text that follows it. Avoid Times 10 point, and don't condense spacing between letters.

2. Be consistent about the placement of section headings. You can pull the resume reader's eye to your name by centering it on the page. Your name and address can go directly underneath. If you are listing more than one address, you may want to put one of the left side and one on the right (and indicate the dates when you will be reachable at each one).

Because we read from left to right, it makes aesthetic and practical sense to position all your headings flush left. Centering headings is a less desirable option but sometimes makes for more visual appeal.

Another consistency rule: Indent entries under all subheadings the same amount of space. (You may want to further indent a second or wraparound line.)

3. Keep graphic elements minimal. To highlight section headings, use all capital letter, boldface, or a slightly larger font size—so long as the letters don't touch each other. To make sure that your resume can be easily scanned, avoid using italics, underlining, reverse lettering, shadowing, or vertical or horizontal lines.

Each entry under a subheading (job, education, activity, functional area) should be indented and/or set off with a simple graphic element so that the eye moves quickly and easily down the page. (Blocks of copy that use only periods as punctuation are more difficult to read.)

Bullets or hyphens are a good way to introduce items under headings.

Example (Functional Resume)

- Provided commentary for audiovisual and multimedia slide shows, ranging in length from 5 to 30 minutes

- Moderated panel discussions of experts, including members of Congress, religious leaders, and college presidents

Bullets are best, but dashes, triangles, or squares are fine, too. You should, however, avoid the temptation to use the many icons and symbols that software makes available—snowflakes, stars, a pointing finger. They detract from the simplicity and form of a resume and are likely to be misread by an optical scanner.

Using a border to frame your copy is a no-no, say graphic designers; it pulls the eye of the reader away from the text, which should be the main attraction. And once again, it can be misread by scanners.

4. Build in white spaces. The easiest way to make sure your resume does not look too cluttered is to allow a 1-inch margin on all four sides and to create what's known in design as leading or extra space between your headings. The widest leading should be between your identification section and your first heading (Work Experience or Education).

If you have plenty of white space, it's preferable to have more space at the bottom than the top. Do not increase the leading between headings or your resume will have a spread-out look.

If you are trying to get more words on a particular page, try reducing your margins or point size. Avoid using a Times 10-point typeface because it cannot be easily read by scanners.

5. Make a sophisticated paper choice. There are three elements to consider: weight, finish, and color. The most commonly used resume papers are 20 lb. bond or 50 lb. offset (both weigh the same despite the difference in lbs.) in a linen (textured) or laid (flat) finish.

If you want that Mercedes-Benz of the paper world, go for a 24 lb. Nekoosa, Classic Linen, or Becket Cambric. A 24 lb. paper is thicker and has more texture than its lighter 20 lb. bond or 50 lb. offset cousins. But keep in mind that using high-quality paper is only important if the resume is being reviewed by a person.

Don't go overboard in your search for a paper that will stand out from the crowd. A heavy cover stock or a gloss finish, for example, will stand out but for the wrong reasons. Neither should you use a colored paper. In the past, using a beige or gray paper was fine. Now that optical scanners are being used, however, it's smart to use white paper because the greater the contrast, the more easily the scanner recognizes characters.

The best way to decide on a paper is to ask your local copy shop to show you the ones mentioned above or other similar papers. You should buy extra sheets of the same paper to use for cover letters; envelopes should also match.

6. Print out and reproduce your resume so that each one looks like an original. Each resume you send out should feature type that is dark and crisp. Laser printers do the best job, although high-quality ink jet printers can also do an acceptable job. Don't use a dot matrix printer; the type is not jagged, which

makes it hard to read, whether it's being screened by a person or scanned by a machine. If you are using a typewriter, use a new ribbon. If you do not have easy access to a good printer, reproduce your original at a copy shop with a high-quality professional copier.

FINAL DESIGN DOS AND DON'TS

- DO strive for consistency in your use of graphic elements. For example, if you capitalized your first job title, subsequent job titles should also be capitalized.

- DON'T mix typefaces.

- DO use black ink.

- DON'T produce a two- or four-color resume to show off your design repertoire.

- DO proofread the final copy several times (and have someone else whose judgment you trust do the same) BEFORE you print out the final version.

- DON'T use screened images behind the type.

- DO put your name on a line of its own at the top of each page of your resume.

- DON'T include a photograph unless you are an actor or actress.

- DON'T fold or staple your resume (it may make it difficult to be fed into a scanner). Instead, send it in an 8½″ × 11″ envelope, and use paper clips.

A WORD ON UNIQUE RESUMES

Yes, they can get an employer's attention. And sometimes they favorably impress an employer. But the arguments against trying to create a unique resume are powerful. (1) Unless you have graphic design training, your efforts are likely to look amateurish; (2) Your unique design (an oversize resume, for example) may prove problematic because it does not easily fit in a resume stack. Set aside, it may be forgotten or trashed; (3) Your attempt to be clever, avant garde, or humorous may be misinterpreted by many; and (4) Many graphic elements, unusual type, or a columnar format can be misread by a scanner (or may be unable to be scanned at all).

Instead of devoting time to making your resume look different, invest it instead in identifying potential employers, meeting with people in those organizations who are in a position to advise or help you, and posting your resume on appropriate databases.

11 ▶ PUT YOUR RESUME TO WORK

Once you have the final version of your resume in hand, you will be armed with your most important job hunting tool: You. Now that you have analyzed your skills and accomplishments on paper, you should feel more confident discussing them with potential employers.

Based on dozens of interviews with employers, recruiters, employment counselors, and job hunters, I believe that a well-written resume can be extremely helpful in your job search, whether it is used to get an interview, familiarize or remind those involved in the hiring process who you are, or to follow up an interview. And with technology making possible new ways to get your resume screened by employers, it's more important than ever to have an up-to-date summary of who you are and what you can do.

HOW TECHNOLOGY IS CHANGING THE WAY RESUMES ARE PROCESSED

Most resumes are still read by people, but in the not-too-distant future, that may change. Already, some large companies (many, but not all of them, high-tech companies) are using automated candidate tracking systems to expedite and improve the hiring process. "It costs most companies an average of $7,500 and takes an average of fifty-four days to find the right person for a job opening," says Gregory Morse, corporate marketing manager for Restrac, maker of automated staffing systems in Dedham, Massachusetts. By using the computer hardware and software made by companies like Restrac, employers can cut their cost per hire and find a suitable match in a much shorter period of time.

Here's how automated candidate tracking systems work. You send your resume to an employer for whom you'd like to work. It might be in response to a help-wanted ad or a position you've seen posted on the World Wide Web, or it may simply be an employer you have targeted through your networking or research. If your resume is received by fax or by conventional mail or delivery, the image is electronically captured by a scanner and sent to a computer equipped with optical character recognition software. The software then converts the information on the resume into a universal computer language called ASCII. If you have sent your resume via e-mail, it is probably already in an ASCII format and is simply sent to the company's database.

When a position becomes available, the hiring manager or the human resources manager selects words that describe the necessary qualifications and other desirable background factors. Some candidate-search programs also ask employers to rate the importance of the qualifications and other factors they specify. For example, an employer may select the following five sets of words as the most critical qualifications: *M.B.A.* (Master of Business Administration), *Stanford University, consumer goods, marketing,* and *product manager.* But other desirable qualifications may also be selected—for example, *Levi Strauss, California,* or functional skills such as *forecasting, budget analysis,* and *direct marketing.* The software then searches all the resumes in the database for these words (they're sometimes referred to as "key words"). What kinds of words are most likely to be key words? They include the following:

- Specific industry
- Job titles
- Specific job skills
- Areas of functional expertise
- Name of a university
- Name of an academic program
- City or state (to identify candidates who are already living in an area or who are willing to relocate)
- Software programs or programming languages
- Computer or other types of equipment
- Name of a professional organization

Resume search software is able to understand context. For example, just because you have the word *Stanford* on your resume doesn't necessarily mean the computer will think you went to Stanford. It understands that Stanford Street or Stanford Heating and Plumbing are different entities than Stanford University. How does it make that judgment? The program looks for other nearby words to establish the proper context. So in the Stanford example, the program would look for the word *university* or a degree (*B.S., B.A., M.B.A., Ph.D.,* etc.) that appeared close to the word *Stanford.*

Some software search engines, such as the one used by Resumix, Inc., which produces human skills management software, are able to interpret key words in relation to a job field. In other words, a candidate whose career is in technology marketing might share some of the same skills or even job responsibilities that a systems analyst has, but the search program has enough intelligence to discern the difference—it would not make the mistake of selecting his resume in a search for a systems analyst despite the fact that a number of words on his resume match the designated key words.

The computer usually ranks the resumes it has selected by assigning greater value to resumes that have the most highly desirable qualifications (as specified by the employer). These top resumes then go to humans, who can better judge whether they are, in fact, candidates who ought to be pursued further.

Is having your resume screened by a computer good news . . . or bad? "You're far better off having your resume screened by a computer than having a person who may or may not be qualified to judge its merits spend less than a minute making the decision of whether or not you're a potential candidate who should be called or interviewed," says Joseph Hnilo, vice president of Resumix. "Even better, if you aren't the right person for the position that's open, you will automatically be considered for future ones, and because it's in a computer database, your resume won't be lost or misplaced."

Another advantage: Your resume will get as much attention as everyone else's, even if it's not as visually pleasing. In fact, plain vanilla resumes—ones that do not use fancy type or graphic elements, including underlining, boldfacing, italics, or reverse lettering—are more likely to be scanned accurately than those that do. When employers see the resumes of top candidates, they usually see what's called the ASCII text version of the resume—same-size type in a conventional font without any frills. While some electronic resume processing systems store an electronic image of the actual resume (and cover letter), that's not usually the one the employer sees. The bottom line: Content is king.

Some people who have written about these technological developments have urged resume writers to create key word summaries at the top of their resumes and to use key words throughout so that their resumes receive a higher "score." I asked the makers of automated tracking systems whether either tactic was necessary or advisable. The answer: No. Here's why: The location of critical words (that describe your job titles, employers, skills, and accomplishments) is irrelevant; the software finds them wherever they are, whether your resume is one page or longer. And once you mention a critical skill, the computer has duly noted it. It's not the repetition of that word or a similar one that will earn you points; it's that skill coupled with other qualifications the employer has specified that will boost you into the circle of "must be considered" candidates. "In the same way that you cannot make up skills or responsibilities to come across as a better candidate to a human reviewing a resume, you cannot manipulate language to fool a computer into thinking you're a better candidate than you really are," says Restrac's Morse.

Another frequently given piece of advice is to eliminate action words that are a staple of traditional resumes. While it's true that the verb is not likely to be a key word (nouns are more likely to be key words), there's no harm in using it to convey a skill or accomplishment. And the fact of the matter is that omitting a verb may make it more difficult for the human reader to understand what you're saying.

How do you know if your resume is going to be screened by a machine or by a human? You don't. There's no harm in asking a company recruiter or human resources department. But the only thing you might do differently is to send a more visually pleasing version of your resume if you know that no automated candidate-tracking system is involved. It always pays to send a cover letter; it will be scanned along with your resume, searched for critical words, and filed in an electronic folder in the event a hiring manager or human resources professional wants to read it.

JOB SURFING IN CYBERSPACE

Just as employers are using technology to help them process job candidates, you can use technology to scout job openings, advertise your availability, and get your resume into the hands of decision makers. While it's more convenient to job surf in cyberspace using your own computer, you don't necessarily need to have a computer, modem, and Internet connection to do so. Some university and public libraries have the necessary equipment and give enrolled students or, in the case of libraries, the general public access to cyberspace. You may be able to walk into your local Kinko's (some of which are open 24 hours a day) and use its computers to job surf. Kinko's Internet service is included in the $12 hourly rate the store charges for computer usage. (At the time this book was being written, Internet services were debuting at a select number of the 227 Kinko's stores nationwide.)

Why extend your job search to cyberspace? Because there are unique opportunities to advertise your availability and to locate openings you may not otherwise learn about.

Just what kind of job openings can be found in cyberspace? It's true that many are targeted to job hunters with skills that fit the needs of high-tech companies (including professionals in areas such as finance, management, human resources, etc.). But every day, companies in a variety of industries are establishing a presence on the World Wide Web and discovering that they, too, can locate potential employees in cyberspace.

If you already have a list of employers you'd like to work for, it's a good idea to see if they have a Web page site. You can learn a lot about a company's products and services, the location of plants and offices, and even what types of job opportunities are available. Some companies post job openings on their home pages; many are likely to be for people whose job skills and experience are Internet or high-tech related. You can usually locate a company's Web site by typing in the company name or acronym after the **http://www**. Follow it with **.com** if it's a for-profit company, **.org** if it's a nonprofit organization, **.gov** if it's a government agency or entity, and **.edu** if it's an educational institution. It's a good idea to convert your resume to an ASCII file so that you can telecommunicate it to an employer who indicates that such a delivery is welcome.

ON-LINE RESUME PREPARATION SERVICES

They're springing up almost as quickly as job Web sites. The service they provide is similar to traditional resume services; they'll help you create a resume and post it on-line. Some also offer the service of creating your own Web page, which requires using HTML (hypertext markup language). Many charge a resume preparation fee (it can be as little as $35 or as high as $175); some charge fees for posting it on-line, some don't.

Do you need such a service? If you don't have easy access to the Internet, using such a service is a way to launch you resume into cyberspace, albeit on the Web site of the resume service, which may or may not attract the kind of employers for whom you hope to work. Some resume services are highly specialized—for example, **Actors Pavilion (http://www.ios.com/~unisoft/ act.html)**, where actors can post resumes and head shots for free. Again, it's important to keep in mind that outside the computer or related high-tech industries, the number of employers who regularly surf the Net in quest of potential employees is still small. As writer Scott Grusky pointed out in "Winning Resume," his *Internet World* article, ". . . when it comes to getting attention, cyberspace is just as cold and cruel a world as the physical domain . . . (what matters is) why you post, where you post, and how you post."

Clearly, if you hope to land a job that is in any way related to the Internet, whether it's designing Web pages, developing innovative customer service strategies or advertising, or establishing revenue opportunities using the Internet, it's smart to advertise yourself with a good-looking home page. If you don't know HTML (and don't have the time or interest to learn this fairly straightforward coding system), you can use the services of an on-line resume service or any company that does Web page design. Make sure that you understand how their pricing is structured and that you like the look of other pages they've produced before you plunk down your money.

JOB-RELATED WEB SITES

The number of career and job-related Web sites is growing every day. Here are some of the more established ones. You'll find that every site you visit provides links to other job sites. Descriptions of each site follow its URL address.

Career Mosaic (http://www.careermosaic.com) You can get profiles (including job listings) of companies—many high tech but others in health care, finance, retailing, and communications, to name a few—you may want to contact.

CareerPath (http://www.careerpath.com) is a job-listings service that provides access to major newspapers' help-wanted advertisements. There is currently no charge for browsing these ads.

E-Span's Interactive Employment Network (http://www.espan.com) You can browse its database of job postings by key words and store your resume so that you can easily respond on-line to job postings. If you register, you only have to log in your search criteria (what job requirements matter to you) once. The system will bring up your profile information each time you log on. You can search for jobs by: key words, company name, geographic location, educational level, years of experience, job level, and salary desired.

Intellimatch (http://www.intellimatch.com) is an on-line human resources service. Its database is primarily technical and engineering, sales and marketing, management, and finance and administration professionals. You can post your resume for free by filling in its WATSON structure resume software. You can download the software, or fill out a paper version of WATSON and mail or fax it back. (To get a paper version, call 1-800-964-6282.) Employers who want to search the database fill in a HOLMES search profile (which describes the type of candidate they're looking for.) If an employer selects your resume, you will be contacted and asked whether you want to release your name and contact information.

JobSource (http://www.jobsource.com) You can check out the job postings by typing in a job title. This site also allows you to view employer profiles and has a feature entitled "Resume Generator" that will guide you through the process of creating or updating an on-line resume.

The Monster Board (http://www.monster.com) Take a "surfari" as this job marketplace with a sense of humor advises, and you'll be able to check out tens of thousands of job opportunities by accessing its database by location, discipline, company, and job title. Career Search is the place to head if you're looking for a job. You can post your resume on-line in Resume City; it will remain active for one year. You can enter a list of companies that are not allowed to see your resume (for example, your current employer). To take a virtual tour of hundreds of corporations, go to Employer Profiles. In the Career Center area, you can find out about job fairs and the companies who will be there (many are high tech), ask career-related questions, and find out about other job Web sites.

Online Career Center (http://occ.com) is a job and resume database managed by a small nonprofit association of employers and top recruitment advertising agencies. There's no charge to you to review the job listings, retrieve company information and profiles, or get various types of career information. Job openings are pulled from a variety of sources, including Internet newsgroups. You can download your resume into the database (keep in mind that your name and contact information will appear for all to see). Only the employers who are OCC members are allowed to access the resume database. If you do not have a computer, you can send your typed resume to: Online Resume Service, 1713 Hemlock Lane, Plainfield, Indiana 46168. It will be input into the computer database for a fee of $6 for three pages and $1.50 for each page thereafter.

For more information about on-line job hunting, get *Be Your Own Headhunter* by Pam Dixon and Sylvia Tiersten (Random House) or *The On-Line Job Search Companion* by James C. Gonyea (McGraw-Hill).

Identify People Who Can Help Circulate Your Resume

You are likely to land more interviews if you identify companies, divisions, departments, and people who have a need for someone with your skills and background. The best place to start is by contacting people who are in a position to provide information about job leads and the hiring process at their companies and put you in touch with those who have the power to hire you.

Now you can begin writing cover letters.

THE SECRETS OF A SUCCESSFUL COVER LETTER

Sending a resume without an accompanying letter is like giving a gift without a card—it's incomplete and can be confusing. You stand a much better chance of being invited to come in for an interview if you take the trouble to briefly explain why you are writing to a particular employer, provided the employer (and not an optical scanner) is "reading" your letter.

If, like most job hunters, you find the prospect of writing a cover letter intimidating, the following suggestions can make the process simpler:

Write to a specific person. It's usually better to target someone within the department you would like to work for who has the power to hire than it is to send your letter to someone in the human resources department. A manager receives far fewer resumes and is more likely to at least skim yours even if he or she is not currently hiring. Even if it ends up getting passed back to human resources, it may get more attention if the manager attaches a positive comment on a note to the human resources director. (If you know that the company you're writing to uses an automated applicant-tracking system, it's a good idea to also send a copy of just your resume to the human resources department so that it will be scanned and added to the company's database of prospective candidates.)

Explain your interest. In the first paragraph, mention how you heard about the job opening or why you are interested in applying for a job with the company.

Try to be as specific as you can—say that you saw the company's ad, that a mutual friend recommended you contact the person, that an employee told you about plans for expansion. (Be sure to name people you refer to but get their permission beforehand.) If possible, discuss why your skills or experience could help the company make progress in areas it has targeted for problem solving or growth.

Avoid using phrases that sound canned or disingenuous—for example, "your xyz department is the best one in the industry," or "working for a company with your excellent reputation." Instead, briefly explain how your interests relate to the products or services of the employer. For example, you might write: "Having been an amateur astronomer since high school, I would welcome the opportunity to use my promotional skills in the public relations department of the planetarium."

Describe your credentials. Don't "lift" parts of your resume and insert them into the cover letter; instead, decide which skills, accomplishments, or experiences are particularly relevant to what the employer is looking for. Then describe them, incorporating, if possible, terminology the employer has used in a help-wanted ad, written job description, or conversation. It's a good idea to refer back to your fact sheets or working draft of your resume to get ideas on language or details worth incorporating.

If, for example, the employer is looking for a sales professional with at least one year's experience in office equipment markets, you might say, "After completing a six-month training program, I competed with experienced salespeople in the competitive computer hardware business and was name second-runner-up in the 'Top Salesperson of the Year' award among a sales force of fifty."

Mentioning three key credentials is plenty; after all, the purpose of the cover letter is to pique the interest of the employer.

State what you do for the company. The purpose of this third paragraph is to set you apart as an applicant who understands the employer's needs, not someone who is simply looking to better his or her own situation. You might say, for example, "I'm confident that I can use my writing and presentation skills to increase attendance at the planetarium and would be prepared to share my ideas on how that might be done during an interview." Or "I would enjoy the opportunity to put my selling skills to work for a company whose product line I'm already familiar with because of my experience."

The more you understand about the current business situation of an employer you will be talking to, the easier it will be to know how to talk about what you can do for that company. Articles that have been written within the last year about the industry or the employer are the easiest and, often, best sources of information.

If you subscribe to a commercial on-line service such as CompuServe, America Online, Microsoft Network, Prodigy, or GEnie, you may be able to search for magazine and newspaper articles about potential employers (or at least get the particulars of when articles about the employer appeared so that you can then track down the full-length articles from your local library). If you are not a subscriber, use the resources of your local library. You can use standard reference books (some are available on CD-ROM) such as the *Business Periodicals Index, The New York Times Index,* or *The Wall Street Journal Index.*

If the prospective employer is a publicly traded company, get a copy of its annual report (call and request one from the public relations or corporate communications department). Annual reports often describe organization structures and provide photos of office and plant facilities.

Ask for an interview. If you have not already mentioned that you would like a chance to meet in person (as was the case in the planetarium example above), add a sentence that requests an interview. Saying that you have ideas about how to improve the employer's service or product (particularly if you know it has been targeted by the employer as an area of concern) is a good way to couch a request instead of simply stating, "I hope we have an opportunity to meet." You might also indicate when it's easiest to reach you, whether it's all right for the employer to contact you at work, and when you will be following up with a check-in phone call (it's a good idea to make that call within a week of the time the person is likely to receive your letter).

Finally, be sure that the design and look of your cover letter are as professional and inviting as your resume. You can achieve that if you do the following:

- Use the same type and size of paper as you did for your resume. Personal stationery or paper with the letterhead of your current (or past) employer are taboo. Stationery that has your name and address printed on it and that is 8½ × 11 inches is preferable.

- Use the same style typeface as you did on your resume. For a long cover letter, a 10-point typeface looks best; for a short letter, a 12-point typeface is fine.

- Set up your letter using traditional business letter rules. The employer's name and address and the salutation should be flush left. You can align your address, the date, the closing, you name, and your phone number at the center of the page of flush left. The best place for a phone number, should you want to include one, is under your name.

- Don't forget to proofread your letter and, if you are composing it on a computer, use a spell-checking feature, too.

Special Situations That You Should Address in Cover Letters

If you're a recent graduate, skip ahead to the next section, "A Final Word," on page 115. If you have work experience but are wondering whether to include salary information or how to address a work gap, your desire to change careers, or your decision to reenter the workforce, read on.

Responding to a Request for Salary Information

Don't reveal your current salary or salary history unless that information has been specifically requested. It's much better to put off a discussion of salary until you have an opportunity to convince an employer that you're the right person for the job.

If salary information has been requested, you can write that you are looking for a salary that's commensurate with your experience and skills. If you do, however, you run the risk of being eliminated since you haven't provided specific figures, although it's likely that most employers will at least call you if your background matches what they're looking for. The other option is to say what you're currently making. If you know you're being well paid and unlikely to replace what you're currently making, you can say that you are flexible about the salary, provided the job is the right one (or the cost of living is lower that where you are now located). If you feel you are being underpaid (and hope to raise your salary considerably with your next career move), you can indicate that you hope to find a position that will fairly compensate you for your contributions. That will tip the employer off that you're looking for a higher salary but leaves open what that amount will be.

Addressing Work Gaps

If you are unemployed and have been searching unsuccessfully for a job for months rather than weeks, you should address the situation in your cover letter. It would help to explain, for example, that you and twenty-five of your colleagues with virtually identical skills and experience were let go when your employer reorganized. Or say that because you were given a general severance, you have the luxury of waiting for just the right job offer (or have turned down offers that were not quite right).

Another good idea is to emphasize the positive things you did during a work gap—for example, helping out in a family business, playing an active role in your child's school, taking courses or seminars to improve your skills, or learning new software program skills on your own. The bottom line is to reassure the employer that you are a hard-working, upbeat job candidate whom he or she cannot afford to ignore.

Making a Case for Why You're Changing Careers

The more drastic your hoped-for move, the more important it is to provide a rationale for why you're switching gears. First, talk about why you hope to find a different kind of position. If you're burned out by the demands of your profession, it's fine to say so, provided you can do so in a way that will be understood and accepted by someone who may not be familiar with your field. When you do, make sure your message doesn't sound as if you're a whiner or complainer or someone who is unwilling or unable to handle stress, long hours, or the emotional demands of your work. Make this explanation brief and to the point.

Second, discuss why you now want to work in this field. The more carefully thought-through your decision, the more believable a prospective employer will find it. Focus in particular on why your skills and experiences have prepared you to succeed in the kind of position you hope to find. If you have taken courses or done other things to help you prepare for this transition, mention them.

Third, talk about why the particular employer you're contacting may benefit from hiring someone like you. You might want to say that the perspective, discipline, or knowledge you bring will be an asset in solving problems, coming up with new ideas and approaches, or dealing with clients.

Explaining Your Return to the Work Force

It's a good idea to briefly summarize why you are reentering the job marketplace. In a sentence or two, say why you left—for example, to raise your family, care for an elderly parent, or earn a degree or certification. Then explain activities or organizations you were involved in that kept you in touch with your profession, allowed you to keep your skills up to date, or helped you develop new skills you now hope to use on the job. Finally, say why you are back in the job market now—for example, because your children are now all in school, you have successfully recovered from your illness, or your financial circumstances have necessitated a return. Keep in mind that the tone of your explanation should be positive and self-confident; don't ever come across as being apologetic or regretful about your absence.

Sample Cover Letter 1
(Recent Graduate)

111 Manor Lane
East Hampton, NY 11937
June 1, 199-

Ms. Ellen Goodrill, President
College Media Relations
411 Broad Street
Keene, NH 03431

Dear Ms. Goodrill:

We met briefly last winter when you visited my boss, Helen Stirling, director of Syracuse University's media relations department. One of my projects as an intern in that office was putting together a report documenting local print, radio, and TV stories on the AIDS research being done at the university's microbiology department. I was very impressed with the level of national coverage you later coordinated on the lab's work.

I recently graduated and am looking for a job with a public relations firm serving higher education clients. I feel that I could be an asset to your firm. Why? Having written twenty-five stories for the campus newspaper, I understand how to position and develop a story idea. I know how to research a story and suggest different angles that might be of interest to different audiences. As a customer service representative (summers during college), I developed an engaging phone manner and an ability to deal with all types of people. Of course, I'm willing to take on any responsibilities that come with an entry-level position with your firm.

I plan to be in the Keene area the week of July 1. Would it be possible to set up an appointment? I will call you next week.

Sincerely,

Judd Chasen
(516-555-8709)

Sample Cover Leter 2
(Job Candidate with Experience)

3231 33rd Street, NW
Washington, DC 20028
June 1, 199-

Mr. Dukes Dunphy
Director, Sports Equipment Marketing
XYZ Corporation
111 Third Avenue
New York, NY 10022

Dear Mr. Dunphy:

The recent story about your company's new product offerings in *Crain's New York Business* caught my attention. In it, you were quoted as saying that you anticipated adding a staff member or two when you introduce your new line of golf products. I feel that I could help make that launch a success.

Here's why: I have been an avid golfer for twenty years and have won many regional tournaments. Beyond that, I have ten years of experience as a marketing specialist with a computer electronics retailer. How can a guy with marketing expertise in a different product line do a good job for you? Let me answer with a brief description of a recent accomplishment.

One year ago, the CEO of my company invited all senior managers to submit ideas on how to increase our store's visibility and image, particularly among 35- to 45-year-old men. My idea, a products/store promotional tie-in with ten sporting events (including two golf tournaments) in the metropolitan area, was implemented with great success. We were able to measure increased store visits (50 percent in the two-week period measured) and increased sales (35 percent) with a coupon that was part of our sports program giveaway.

I feel that I can get similar results with your new product line. I will call you within the week to find out if we can arrange a time to talk.

Sincerely,

Dale Robinson
(202-555-1987)

A Final Word

I hope that you feel confident and optimistic about starting your job search as a result of reading *The New 90-Minute Resume* and working through the process. Keep in mind that finding the right job may take you weeks or even months of looking. If you are not successful in getting interviews, you many have to become more aggressive in tracking down leads (by talking to as many "connected" people as you can about what you are looking for). Or you may have to expand your geographic or career boundaries.

Don't get discouraged if you get rejection after rejection. You need only one "Yes" to get a new job. And the more "No's" you hear, the better the odds that it won't be long before you get a "Yes."

12 ▶ 90-MINUTE RESULTS

The sample resumes that appear in this section have been adapted from real resumes. Each is depicted before and after the job hunter went through the 90-minute process, and analyses of the biggest faults of the "Before" version and the strong points of the "After" version are provided.

DIRECTORY OF RESUME MAKEOVERS

The Chronological Format

The chronological format is the most readily understood and reader-friendly resume format. In a chronological resume, your work experience is arranged in a timeline, starting with your most recent job and working back from there. Job titles, names of employers, and dates of employment are easier to identify with this format, making it a favorite among employment agency counselors, executive recruiters, and human resources personnel. Also, the placement of dates next to facts makes reference information easier to verify.

Resume of a Recent Graduate

Nancy Baxter majored in biology in college and wants to work full-time as a research assistant at a laboratory before starting her graduate studies.

Weaknesses in the "Before" version:

- Preferable to center personal identification information
- Script typeface hard to read; too casual looking
- Uses abbreviations that may not be recognized
- Education section should precede work experience section
- Insufficient detail about job responsibilities
- Too skeletal overall

Improvements in the "After" version:

- Typeface (Times Roman) and design more professional looking
- Separating work experience into two sections helpful
- Addition of numbers helps fill out scope of her work
- More detailed descriptions of job responsibilities
- Accomplishments make work experience, activities, and interests stronger

Before

NANCY BAXTER
305 Channing Way
Berkeley, CA 94704
415-555-0985

WORK EXPERIENCE

Laboratory Assistant, Genetics Laboratory, UC, Berkeley, 1994–96 (15 hours a week during school term)

— Prepared media and solutions, which involved use of pH meter

— Cared for lab animals

— Conducted supply and chemical inventories

Assistant Laboratory Manager, JDL Laboratories, Summers 1993–95

— Helped research new lab equipment

— Supervised daily lab clean-up

— Helped plan schedules for research work projects

Tennis Instructor, Claremont Racquet Club, Summers 1990–92

EDUCATION

B.S., Biology, UC, 1996, Magna Cum Laude

ACTIVITIES

Coordinator, Speakers' Forum, Student Science Forum, 1995–96

— Researched and contacted prominent scientists to participate in panel discussions

INTERESTS

Tennis and photography

After

Nancy Baxter
305 Channing Way
Berkeley, CA 94704
415-555-0985

EDUCATION   B.S., Biology, University of California at Berkeley

SKILLS   Lab protocols, research animal care, lab equipment maintenance, safe handling of lab chemicals and materials

LABORATORY WORK EXPERIENCE

1994–1996
(part-time)   Laboratory Assistant, Biology Laboratory, University of California at Berkeley

- Selected for lab fellowship on basis of grade point average and "potential for success in science"
- Prepared media and solutions, which involved use of pH meter
- Cared for over 200 laboratory animals, including mice, rats, and rabbits
- Conducted supply and chemical inventories

Summers
1992–1994   Assistant Laboratory Manager, JDL Laboratories, San Francisco, California

- Presented results of research on new lab equipment totaling $50,000, which was subsequently approved and purchased
- Supervised daily lab clean-up; made sure standards of cleanliness were met
- Drew up preliminary reports for personnel and supplies needed for upcoming research projects

ADDITIONAL WORK EXPERIENCE

Summers
1990–1992   Tennis Instructor, Claremont Racquet Club

ACTIVITIES   Coordinator, Speakers Forum, Student Science Forum, 1995–1996

Researched and contacted prominent scientists to participate in five panel discussions on "hot" scientific issues, events drew audiences of 200+

INTERESTS   Public speaking (have given two dozen presentations about careers in science to high school students in 1995 and 1996); skiing

Resume of a Job Candidate with Experience

Paula has worked for eight years in management capacities in different types of restaurants. Her job target is to find a job as manager of a large restaurant in a major hotel chain in a resort setting.

Weaknesses in the "Before" version:

- Unsophisticated typeface
- Hard-to-read blocks of copy
- Not enough numbers
- No mention of accomplishments or results

Improvements in the "After" version:

- Classy typeface (Bauer Bodoni)
- Better spacing, including dates of employment that are easy to spot
- Greater use of numbers
- Accomplishments are described, often featuring bottom-line results
- Less important job tasks omitted
- Interests section with good detail provided

Before

Paula Sawbridge
6666 Coleridge Avenue
Palo Alto, California 94022
415-555-9234

PROFESSIONAL HISTORY
1993–present
Food & Beverage Manager, Marriott Corporation, Palo Alto, California

Institution food service manager for corporate conference center responsible for budgets, personnel, purchasing, and cost control. Revamped menus, product merchandising, and promotions opening the facility to new sources of revenue. Directed all areas of operation of 350-seat dining room, lounge, and catering. Coordinated summer internship program, employee cross-training, and program for handicapped adults. Wrote department standard operating procedures manual.

1990–1993
Manager, Ship Ahoy Restaurant, Milwaukee, Wisconsin

Supervised dining room and staff; coordinated advertising; managed group sales, special events, and promotions for this floating-barge restaurant. Initiated campaign to increase check averages through employee training and beverage promotions.

1988–1990
Manager, Giovanni's Restaurant, Hilton Head Island, South Carolina

Supervised operation of 150-seat restaurant and directed opening of New York-style catering business in second outlet. Coordinated advertising, generated press releases and special event promotions. Developed new marketing plan and budget.

1986–1988
Assistant Manager, Winberie's Restaurant (Stouffer Restaurant Company), Denver, Colorado

Assisted in management of operation of 150-seat restaurant. Helped train twenty new employees. Developed weekly schedule for thirty employees and resolved scheduling problems. Helped oversee major kitchen remodeling.

EDUCATION

B.A., 1986, University of Massachusetts at Amherst
Major: Hotel and restaurant management

After

Paula Sawbridge
6666 Coleridge Avenue
Palo Alto, California 94022
415-555-9234

PROFESSIONAL EXPERIENCE

1993–present   Food & Beverage Manager, Marriott Corporation, Palo Alto, California

- Direct all areas of operation of 350-seat dining room, lounge, and catering service, including budgets, personnel, purchasing, and cost control
- Introduced staff training programs to improve service and spa cuisine menu, both of which played major roles in increasing business 20 percent during my tenure
- Convinced management to back a $25,000 promotion aimed at foreign companies doing business in the Bay Area, resulting in fifteen new clients
- Coordinated summer internship program, and program for handicapped adults, five new hires resulted; all have since been recognized as employees of the month

1990–1993   Manager, Ship Ahoy Restaurant, Milwaukee, Wisconsin

- Supervised twenty-five staff members who served three dining rooms seating 250
- Coordinated advertising, managed group sales, special events, and promotions for this floating-barge restaurant, resulting in 15 percent increase in business annually
- Initiated campaign to increase check averages through employee training and beverage promotions; daily averages rose $30 per employee

1988–1990   Manager, Giovanni's Restaurant, Hilton Head Island, South Carolina

- Supervised operation of 150-seat restaurant
- Directed opening of New York-style catering business, which added 10 percent annually to restaurant profits
- Developed new marketing plan, which helped increase lunch business 25 percent

1986–1988   Assistant Manager, Winberie's Restaurant (Stouffer Restaurant Company), Denver, Colorado

- Assisted in management of operation of 150-seat restaurant
- Helped train twenty new employees in service, bartending, and busing skills
- Developed weekly schedule for thirty employees
- Helped oversee $100,000 major kitchen reconstruction

EDUCATION
1986, B.A., Hotel and Restaurant Management, University of Massachusetts at Amherst

INTERESTS
Bicycling (elected chair of community biking organization; currently serving two-year term; initiated successful local ballot issue for development of additional bike lanes)

Resume of a Job Candidate Changing Careers

John has been working as a coach and athletic director since playing basketball during college. He recently earned an M.B.A. and would like to combine his interest in sports with his business degree.

Weaknesses in the "Before" version:

- Amateurish look
- Arrangement of personal information could be misread by scanner
- Does not reflect marketing background
- Job tasks read as if they've been lifted from a personnel manual
- No attention is given to results or accomplishments

Improvements in the "After" version:

- Typeface (News Gothic) more readable
- Clean, easy-to-read look
- Summary is strong where-I've-been/where-I-want-to-go statement
- Number details add credibility
- Emphasis on accomplishments (increased motivation, better attendance, additional revenue) that are understood and important in business world

Before

John Jacobson   44 Wittenberg Road Oxford, Ohio 43590
     513-555-0987 (h)   513-555-9000 (w)

Job Objective: A position in sports management

Education: 1996, M.B.A., Miami University
            1982, B.S., Marketing, Michigan State University

Work Experience:

Miami University, Oxford, Ohio
DIRECTOR OF INTERCOLLEGIATE ATHLETICS, 1990-present

—Responsible for operation of entire athletic program
—Prepare annual athletic and student activities budgets
—Hire, evaluate, and supervise coaches and intramural staff
—Determine eligibility in accordance with NJCAA regulations
—Arrange payroll disbursements for staff

Baldwin-Wallace College, Berea, Ohio
ASSISTANT DIRECTOR OF ATHLETICS, 1986-1990

—Assisted director in operation of entire athletic program
—Helped hire and supervise coaches and intramural staff
—Purchased uniforms, equipment, and supplies
—Scheduled maintenance of fields, gym set-ups, and clean-ups
—Acted as head coach for basketball team

University of Toledo, Toledo, Ohio
HEAD BASKETBALL COACH, 1978-1982

—Recruited promising high school players for team
—Led team through four winning seasons
—Arranged conference schedules

Personal Sports Involvement:
Forward, Michigan State University Spartans, 1980-82
Cyclist (changed sports after 1978 knee injury); have participated
in 100 cycling events in last fourteen years

After

John Jacobson

44 Wittenberg Road   513-555-0987 (h)
Oxford, Ohio 43590   513-555-9000 (w)

SUMMARY

As a college-level sports director for eighteen years, I have managed and promoted successful athletic programs. With my newly-earned M.B.A. degree, I want to put my marketing skills to work for a sports manufacturer.

EDUCATION

1996, M.B.A., Miami University, Oxford, Ohio

1982, B.S., Marketing, Michigan State University

WORK EXPERIENCE

**Director of Intercollegiate Athletics, 1990–present
Miami University**

- Direct athletic program, which produced annual revenues of $2 million and operated on a $1-million budget
- Supervise 25-member coaching staff, who have collectively improved their team's win/loss records by 25 percent
- Increased attendance at athletic events in 1994–95 school year by 20 percent to highest levels in school's history
- Played a major role in development of new $3-million sports facility on campus

**Assistant Director of Athletics, 1986–1990
Baldwin-Wallace College, Berea, Ohio**

- Helped coordinate an athletic program that featured three intramural teams and twenty-five intramural programs
- Evaluated and made hiring recommendations for three coaching positions
- Purchased uniforms, equipment, and supplies
- Scheduled maintenance of fields, gym set-ups, and clean-ups
- Determined player eligibility

**Head Basketball Coach, 1982-1986
University of Toledo, Toledo, Ohio**

- Recruited players with academic and athletic potential
- Led team through four winning seasons

PERSONAL SPORTS INVOLVEMENT

Forward, Michigan State University Spartans, 1980-1982

Cyclist; have participated in 100 cycling events in last fourteen years

---

Resume of a Job Candidate Changing Industries

Jack has developed marketing expertise by working for three different types of manufacturers. He hopes to change industries again. His resume needs to reflect his versatility and his ability to quickly absorb product information and understand a market.

Weaknesses in the "Before" version:

- Personal information should be centered
- Blocks of copy make it more difficult to read
- Type size does not vary, giving resume a boring look
- Job target would be helpful
- Information about job tasks too sketchy
- No description of accomplishments
- No mention of the product lines he handled
- Uses first person and complete sentences (takes up a lot of space unnecessarily)

Improvements in the "After" version:

- Typeface (Helvetica) sharper
- Clear identification of job title
- Description of companies helpful
- Addition of job target
- Separate bulleted items make reading easier
- Details of accomplishments and results greatly enhance resume's strength

Before

Jack Robertson
6889 Cranberry Road
Philadelphia, Pennsylvania 67891
215-555-2220

MARKETING EXPERIENCE

10/92–present   Doyle Chemical Products, Trenton, NJ

As senior marketing representative, I interact with business area managers, assisting in the planning of marketing efforts and executing all communications programs, including advertising, trade shows, and sales promotions.

8/90–10/92   Household Paper Manufacturers, Newark, NJ

As a marketing specialist, I was responsible for overseeing the creative design and implementation of advertising, product promotions, sales brochures, direct mail, and field sales communications. Worked directly with product managers in planning and implementing new product introductions.

6/85–8/90   Saxon Enterprises, Princeton, NJ

As product manager, I was responsible for all phases of product development, including determining market needs, defining product requirements, negotiating functional specifications, planning product introductions, and initiating sales support.

EDUCATION   B.S., May 1985, Rutgers University, New Brunswick, NJ

Major: Marketing

Grade Point Average: 3.5

ACTIVITIES   Vice President, New Jersey Regional Chapter, Association of Marketing Professionals, 1994–1996

INTERESTS   Woodworking, cabinetry

After

Jack Robertson
6889 Cranberry Road
Philadelphia, Pennsylvania 67891
215-555-2220

JOB TARGET   A senior marketing position with a company whose product line includes carpentry tools, cabinets, or home improvement services

MARKETING EXPERIENCE

10/92–present   Senior Marketing Representative

Doyle Chemical Products, Trenton, NJ ($2.5-billion chemical manufacturer)

—Have contributed to overall company profit increases averaging 15 percent a year for three years (10 percent higher than five years preceding my tenure)

—Work with five division heads to formulate marketing strategies for each product area, a teamwork approach I introduced

—Instituted new product promotions with customers, which included samples, an innovation that prompted increased orders and compliments from customers

8/90–10/92   Marketing Specialist

Household Paper Manufacturers, Newark, NJ ($250-million paper product manufacturer)

—Introduced new paper towel line, which has captured a 5 percent market share since its inception

—Oversaw design and implementation of advertising, product promotions, sales brochures, direct mail, and field sales communications for twenty-five products

—Conducted research that convinced senior management to reposition three products, all of which saw sales increases of 5–10 percent in 1992

6/85–8/90   Product Manager, Saxon Enterprises, Princeton, New Jersey ($100-million photo supplies manufacturer)

—Helped launch darkroom products division by surveying market needs, defining product requirements, and negotiating product specifications

—Worked with marketing and sales department to sell new line, which accounted for 10 percent of company's profits after three years

EDUCATION   B.S., May, 1985, Rutgers University, New Brunswick, NJ

ACTIVITIES AND AWARDS

Vice President, New Jersey Regional Chapter, Association of Marketing Professionals, 1994–1996

AMP Marketing Professional of the Year, 1995

INTERESTS   Woodworking, cabinetry (have designed and constructed built-ins in seven rooms of my home, including kitchen)

Resume of a Job Candidate Reentering the Work Force

Natasha took an eight-year leave of absence from her nursing career to be at home with her young children. For the last two years, she has volunteered to work as a school nurse at the elementary school they attend. She wants to find a job on par with the last one she left as the nursing care coordinator of a large hospital.

Weaknesses in the "Before" version:

- "Resume of" unnecessary
- Typeface too casual/hard to read
- Asterisks may be misread by scanner
- Inclusion of job title with name not advisable
- Stating salary desired is not in candidate's best interest
- Some headings too whimsical; others such as "Availability" are unnecessary
- Job responsibilities convey "antiseptic" view of candidate
- Accomplishments/results need to be included

Improvements in the "After" version:

- Typeface (Garamond) more readable and professional-looking
- Summary section strong and more professional than "What I've been doing" and "What I'd like to do" sections
- Inclusion and details of recent volunteer nurse experience valuable addition (shows continuing professional interest/involvement)
- Description of accomplishments helps candidate come across as an innovative manager
- Details of interests provide further understanding of the kind of person the candidate is

Before

Resume of

Natasha Brooks, Nursing Care Coordinator

Contact Information: 125 Glen Oaks Drive, Teaneck, NJ 84320
• 201-555-0043 • fax: 201-555-0044 •
e-mail: NatBr@aol.com

What I'd like to do: Find a supervisory position in a 500+ bed facility

Available: Immediately

Desired salary: $40,000+

What I've been doing: I resigned from my last position in June 1988 to give birth to my first child. I had a second child in August 1990. It has been my choice to be a full-time, at-home mom during this time. I have, however, volunteered to serve as the school nurse on a part-time basis for the last two years.

Nursing experience: St. Mary's Hospital, a 500+ bed facility, Montclair, New Jersey
Nursing Care Coordinator, 1980–1990

* Scheduled unit staffing

* Maintained quality patient care administered according to institutional policies and procedures

* Organized in-service educational meetings on unit

* Wrote annual report and professional goals for unit, staff, and myself

* Resolved unit staffing problems

* Encouraged and motivated staff to participate in furthering their own career paths

* Planned and delegated appropriate patient care assignments

* Communicated new hospital policies and procedures to staff

Assistant Nursing Care Coordinator, 1975–1980

Staff Nurse (Medical/Surgical Unit) 1970–1975

Education: 1980, B.S. Health Care Administration, Fairleigh Dickinson University, Teaneck, New Jersey

1970, B.S. Nursing, Rutgers University, New Brunswick, New Jersey

Professional Affiliations: American Nurses Association
American Management Association
National Association of Female Executives

Interests: Reading, sewing, swimming

After

Natasha Brooks
125 Glen Oaks Drive, Teaneck, NJ 84320
201-555-0043

Summary

Twenty years' experience as a registered nurse in surgical, medical, orthopedic, gynecological, operating room, labor and delivery, and ICU units. Fifteen years' experience in supervisory positions. Spent last eight years at home with my two young children.

Nursing Experience

SCHOOL NURSE, 1994–1996

Thomas Edison Elementary School, Teaneck, New Jersey

- Volunteered 15 hours a week to assist with medical needs of 55-member staff and student population of 350
- Drew up new emergency medical guidelines for faculty and staff to follow in event of playground accidents and illnesses affecting a population of 5–9 year olds, which was approved by the principal and subsequently adopted by three other elementary schools in the district
- Received award from the school superintendent for my role in getting fast emergency care for a student with a rare blood clotting disorder; in the awards, ceremony he said: "Had it not been for the intervention of Natasha Brooks, the student may have bled to death."

NURSING CARE COORDINATOR, 1980–1990

St. Mary's Hospital, Montclair, New Jersey

- Scheduled three nursing shifts of 100 RNs
- Maintained high-quality patient care despite cutbacks in staff through initiation of motivational workshops and innovative time off and patient/scheduling assignment bids for nurses who received excellent performance ratings
- Received award from American Nurses Association for development of performance evaluation/reward system in 1990
- Developed color-coded system for patient charts to facilitate doctors' patient assignments on unit
- Served as grievance chair representing all RN's in contractual disputes; successfully resolved 100 cases over ten-year period
- Contributed and developed five ideas to the joint medical/nursing committee about cost reduction and patient care that were successfully adopted

ASSISTANT NURSING CARE COORDINATOR, 1975–1980

STAFF NURSE (Medical/Surgical Unit) 1970–1975

Education

1980, B.S. Health Care Administration, Fairleigh Dickinson University, Teaneck, New Jersey

1970, B.S. Nursing, Rutgers University, New Brunswick, New Jersey

Professional Affiliations

- American Nurses Association, member, 1970–current
- New Jersey Chapter President, 1985–1987
- American Management Association, member, 1981–1990
- National Association of Female Executives, member, 1985–1990

Interests

Reading mysteries; quilting (have sewn 50 quilts, half of which I donated to auctions to benefit the Ronald McDonald House, a home away from home for families whose children are hospitalized with serious illnesses); swimming (member of local master's swim team)

THE FUNCTIONAL FORMAT

You've already done most of the work needed to create a functional resume. You identified the main areas of expertise required by your job target in "First, Your Fact Sheets," and in "What Are You an Expert At?" you grouped descriptions of tasks and accomplishments from each job or activity related to your target under the appropriate area of expertise. So pull out those work sheets and let's move ahead.

With this format, it's best to use the past tense of all action verbs, even for descriptions of current tasks. After each entry, list the year or years you performed or accomplished it so that the resume reader can quickly determine when you acquired the skill. Next, create a job history section. List your job title, the name of the employer, location (if necessary), and the dates of employment.

EXAMPLE

Indiana University, Bloomington, Indiana, 1988–present
>College Adviser, 1994–present
>Program Assistant, Arts and Sciences Division, 1992–93
>Teaching Assistant, English Department, 1991–92

These two sections—areas of expertise (there should be two to four of them) and work history—are the heart of a functional resume. Follow the directions in "Create a Working Draft" on page 74 for the remaining sections. The sequence should be:

- Identification

- Job Objective or Summary of Qualifications or Key Word Summary (optional)

- Areas of Expertise

- Work History

- Skills (optional)

- Education

- Interests

Resume of a Recent Graduate

Jason is a 1996 graduate who hopes to parlay his fund-raising and coordination skills into a job with a lobbying organization.

Weaknesses in the "Before" version:

- Identification section has too many bullets
- Font size (in ID section disproportionately large)
- Too casual a typeface
- Too skeletal looking
- Centering information unconventional
- Too few details about his responsibilities and accomplishments

Improvements in the "After" version:

- Much improved design and typeface (Futura)
- Functional categories are well chosen
- Details provide much better picture of candidate
- Use of numbers helps reader understand his role and contributions

Before

• Jason Snyder • 38-49 Crescent Street • Bay Village, Ohio • 44039 • 216-555-9854 (as of 6/15/96)
•

EDUCATION

Bachelor of Arts, Speech Communication, Case Western Reserve University, 1996, Cum Laude

ACTIVITIES

Volunteer staff worker, Ohio Gubernatorial Fund-raising, 1992-1994
Worked on a part-time basis making phone calls, asking for campaign donations with mailings, and making arrangements for candidate to visit Ohio colleges

President, Student Activities Board, 1995-1996
Oversaw budget of $700,000, set up new mailing system to students, approved and scheduled forty-five campus events

Student Coordinator, Cuyahoga, Ohio, Health Fair, Summer 1991
Helped raise money and material from local businesses
Found volunteers to help man booths

Student Telethon Volunteer, 1994-1996
Helped raise money for university in telethons

WORK EXPERIENCE

Waiter, The Rusty Scupper, Summers 1992-1995
Served food, assisted food-and-beverage manager with purchase orders, trained new waiters

INTERESTS

Hiking and electoral politics

After

Jason Snyder
38-49 Crescent Street, Bay Village, Ohio 44039
216-555-9854 (as of 6/15/96)

JOB OBJECTIVE A position as a research assistant or grassroots fundraiser with an advocacy group

EDUCATION 1996, Bachelor of Arts, Speech Communication, Case Western Reserve University, University Heights, Ohio

Cum Laude

CAPABILITIES

Fund-raising

Helped raise over $10,000 campaign contributions in successful Ohio 1994 gubernatorial campaign, 1992–1994

Solicited printed materials and $5,000 in donations from corporate sponsors of health fair, 1992

Participated in five telethons sponsored by university alumni office; personally raised $15,000 in pledges, 1993–1996

Administration

Helped plan thirty candidate appearances, including locations and facilities, 1992–1994

Implemented student database, 1995–1996

Authorized expenditure of $700,000 student activities budget, 1995–1996

Management

Mobilized 100 volunteers and coordinated their work at health fair, 1991

Devised system for collection, organization, and dissemination of information to student body of 35,000, 1995–1996

EXPERIENCE 1995–1996 President, Student Activities Board, Case Western Reserve University, University Heights, Ohio

Summers 1992–1995 Waiter, The Rusty Scupper, Lakewood, Ohio

1992–1994 Volunteer Staff Worker, Ohio Gubernatorial Fund-raising, Cleveland, Ohio,

1991 Student Coordinator, Cuyahoga Health Fair, Cuyahoga, Ohio

INTERESTS Hiking the Appalachian Trail

Speaking to grade school students about electoral politics

Resume of a Job Candidate with Experience

Michael has held four positions since graduating from college thirteen years ago. He would like to land a job with a management consulting firm specializing in public-sector clients. With his newly earned M.B.A. and years of experience in city government agencies, he feels that a functional resume would help him make a better case for such a move.

Weaknesses in the "Before" version:

- "Resume of" not necessary
- Clear typeface, but bland overall look
- Identification information poorly spaced; difficult for scanners to process
- Unnecessary use of first person
- Responsibilities read like a job description list
- Lacks details
- No mention of accomplishments
- New job objective would be useful
- Current chronological format doesn't adequately support new job objective

Improvements in the "After" version:

- Same typeface (Helvetica), but use of different type sizes and capitalizations provides more visual zip
- Addition of clearly-stated job objective helpful
- Addition of summary of qualifications provides "at a glance" candidate profile
- Identification of functional areas clear and well thought through
- Introduction of more details and accomplishments lends important credibility
- Selection of bulleted items eliminates repetition of some job tasks
- Inclusion of dates after job tasks/accomplishments provides context and time for when skill last performed
- Addition of M.A. credential is important
- Added detail under interests adds interest

Before

RESUME OF

Michael DeAngelis   202 Balmoray Drive   Durham, North Carolina 77107

phone: 717-555-7812

EXPERIENCE
1992–1996

City Engineer, City of Durham, North Carolina
I reorganized the engineering department into four divisions.
I managed an operating and capital budget of $10M.
I coordinated preparation of the city's five-year capital improvement plan.
I developed self-directed teams to create internal and external policies and procedures.
I came up with design criteria for use by private developers and engineers.
I managed the Johnson Parkway Project.

1989–1992

Assistant to the Director of Public Works, City of Charleston, West Virginia
I was the administrative officer for the Department of Public Works.
I managed the engineering services division responsible for issuing utility connection permits.
I supervised coordination of technical review for aspects of a proposed development.
I prepared department policies and procedures relating to construction and design of public improvements.
I coordinated budget and capital improvement plan preparations.
I was the project manager for two major utility rate studies.

1983–1989

Engineer II: Civil, City of Reading, Pennsylvania
I started as an engineering aide and held five positions prior to being made Engineer II in 1987.
I was the project manager for a major highway department road upgrade program.
I assisted in the development of budgets for major capital improvements.
I supervised the planning, design, consultant coordination, and administration of public facilities including water systems, wastewater systems, and streets.

PROFESSIONAL CREDENTIALS AND ACTIVITIES

Civil Engineer, Pennsylvania, 678143; West Virginia, 087657; North Carolina, C-576439

Vice President, American Public Works Association, Durham Chapter, 1994-96

Fellow, American Society of Civil Engineers

Member, American Water Works Association

EDUCATION

M.B.A., Carnegie-Mellon University, 1989

B.S., Civil Engineering, Carnegie Mellon University, 1983

INTERESTS

Bicycling, Medieval jousting, and reading

After

Michael DeAngelis

202 Balmoray Drive
Durham, North Carolina 77107
717-555-7812

JOB OBJECTIVE To move from the public to the private sector to a managerial position with a management consulting firm specializing in public sector clients

SUMMARY OF QUALIFICATIONS Thirteen years of experience as a civil engineer; seven years of management and fiscal administration; M.B.A., including a Master of Arts in Engineering Management; expertise in project management, budget projects, and clear report writing; reputation for efficiency and working within budget; received citations from management in all jobs held for superlative performance

AREAS OF EXPERTISE
Management

- Managed Johnson Parkway Project, a $2.5M federally funded project; received national Infrastructure Award by *City and County Magazine*, 1995
- Coordinated preparation of the city's five-year capital improvement plan, which was cited by mayor as being principal catalyst behind $10M new business investments by private companies, 1992
- Managed engineering services division; enacted employee suggestions on reducing water meter installation and reduced average installation time by three days, 1992
- Administered 200-employee Department of Public Works; reduced staff by 15 percent through reallocation of job responsibilities and early retirement options, 1990

Fiscal Administration

- Prepared, allocated, and managed an operating and capital budget of $10M, 1996
- Coordinated budget and capital improvement plan preparation of $7M, 1990
- Initiated two major utility rate studies; recommended change that resulted in savings of $1M annually to city, 1990

Employee Supervision

- Developed self-directed teams to create improved policies and procedures for servicing public and internal customer needs; was cited as one of top twenty innovative employee plans by American Management Association, 1995
- Increased organizational efficiency and accountability by reorganizing the engineering department into four divisions—Design, Transportation, Utilities, and Development, 1994

Civil Engineering

- Devised design criteria explaining the City's design standards for public improvements for use by private developers and engineers; reduced processing time by 25 percent, 1993
- Supervised coordination of technical review for water, sewer, storm drain, and street elements aspects of a $5M development
- Served as project manager for a $1M highway department road upgrade program; finished the project two months ahead of schedule, 1986
- Supervised the planning, design, consultant coordination, and administration of public facilities including water systems, wastewater systems, and streets; cited three times for superior performance, 1985–1989

JOB HISTORY

1992–1996   *City Engineer, City of Durham, North Carolina*

1989–1992   *Assistant to the Director of Public Works, City of Charleston, West Virginia*

1983–1989   *Engineer II: Civil, City of Reading, Pennsylvania*
Started as an engineering aide and held five positions prior to being made Engineer II in 1987

EDUCATION

Master of Business Administration, and Master of Arts in Engineering Administration, Carnegie Mellon University, 1989

Bachelor of Science, Civil Engineering, Carnegie Mellon University, 1983

PROFESSIONAL CREDENTIALS AND INVOLVEMENTS

Civil Engineer, Pennsylvania, 678143; West Virginia, 087657; North Carolina, C-576439
Vice President, American Public Works Association, Durham Chapter, 1994–96
Fellow, American Society of Civil Engineers
Member, American Water Works Association

INTERESTS

Bicycling (have competed in over thirty long-distance events)

Medieval jousting (perform at a half dozen Renaissance fairs annually)

Reading mysteries

Resume of a Job Candidate Changing Careers

Marie has been working as a social worker and administrator of social services for twenty years. To supplement her income in the last five years, she has worked part-time as a real estate broker. She now wants to make the switch to private industry in a position as a relocation counselor for a large company.

Weaknesses in the "Before" version:

- Unconventional typeface that may not scan well
- Blocks of copy hard to read
- Too much emphasis on social work experience
- Some numbers; more would be helpful
- No analysis of transferable skills

Improvements in the "After" version:

- Typeface (Palatino) much easier to read
- Each line of identification on its own line
- Addition of summary helpful in explaining career change
- Use of functional skill areas adds credibility/makes it easier for reader to see why she can do the job
- Use of numbers helps quantify achievements
- More detailed analysis of skills and accomplishments useful
- Addition of interests a plus

Before

Marie Jonello

19 Webster Road, N. Miami, Florida, 33138
305-555-9875

OBJECTIVE

A position as a relocation counselor

REAL ESTATE EXPERIENCE

Real Estate Agent, Century 21, Fort Lauderdale, Florida, 1992–present

Handled residential real estate sales. Put in 10 hours a week in services of major companies. Developed client lists. Worked with relocation services of major companies. Sold an average of $1-million worth of homes annually. Built database of 500 clients.

SOCIAL WORK EXPERIENCE

Director, Rosemont Center, Fort Lauderdale, Florida, 1989–present

Total responsibility for this 100-bed inpatient treatment facility for substance abusers. Hired and supervised professional and hourly employees. Devised and directed therapy programs. Personally led five sessions per week. Acted on recommendations of intake counselors; average of five new patients admitted weekly. Introduced posttreatment tracking systems to determine treatment effectiveness. Two-year follow-up showed that 50 percent of patients were active in AA and employed one year after graduating from program.

Substance Abuse Counselor, The Lake Institute, Lorain, Ohio, 1986–1989

Evaluated average of fifteen patients per week and made recommendations on intake. Worked with adult and juvenile patients. Counseled families on how to perform crisis interventions. Successfully coached over 100 families through intervention process. Worked one-on-one and in group counseling sessions with patients. Counseled family members on how to help their loved one after treatment.

Resident Adviser, Evergreen Home for Girls, Cleveland, Ohio, 1981–1986

Supervised twenty delinquent adolescent girls in residential setting. Enforced disciplinary code. Counseled residents one-on-one for emotional, psychological, and substance abuse problems. Encouraged girls to excel in their studies; helped with homework.

Social Worker, City of Pittsburgh, 1975–1982

Supervised a caseload of fifty families. Evaluated living situation and family life to determine appropriate action; made recommendations to supervisory board. Advised clients on rage of services available, including special education programs, disability, and food stamp and welfare benefits.

EDUCATION AND LICENSES

Licensed real estate salesperson, State of Florida, 1992
Real Estate Certificate program, Dade Community College, 1992
M.S.W., Columbia University, 1977
B.A., Hunter College, New York, NY, 1975

After

Marie Jonello
19 Webster Road
N. Miami, Florida, 33138
305-555-9875

Job Objective: A position as a relocation counselor

Summary

As a counseling professional with twenty years of experience and a real estate broker with five years' experience, I can anticipate problems and offer practical housing, education, and other solutions for families being relocated by their companies. Having made five major moves in my adult life, I am sensitive to the adjustments that relocation requires and how to make transitions smoother.

Real Estate

- Averaged $1 million in residential real estate sales a year for past four years, selling part-time
- Specialized in working with relocation services of major companies; found desirable housing situations for twenty clients in last two years
- Have demonstrated a capacity to work with the most difficult and demanding clients, who were referred to me by my office manager because of my ability to work with them

Counseling

- Evaluated clients' problems and concerns by asking questions, listening carefully to answers, and comparing information gathered from close friends, relatives, and employers
- Worked one-on-one and in a group setting to make clients aware of their behavior and its effects on their work, families, and personal lives.
- Received 50 letters from substance abusers in recovery who credit me with playing a major role in their return to sobriety

Administration

- Orchestrated the successful functioning of a facility employing 55 people and treating as many as 100 clients at a time; follow-up surveys indicate program success—50 percent of clients sober and working a year after their "graduation"
- Built a database of 500 clients on computer; by maintaining regular contact, successfully did business with one third

Employment History

Real Estate Agent, Century 21, Fort Lauderdale, Florida, 1992–present
Director, Rosemont Center, Fort Lauderdale, Florida, 1989–present
Substance Abuse Counselor, The Lakeland Institute, Lorain, Ohio, 1986–1989
Resident Adviser, Evergreen Home for Girls, Lexington, Kentucky, 1981–1986
Social Worker, City of Pittsburgh, 1976–1981

Education and Licenses

Licensed real estate salesperson, State of Florida, 1992
Real Estate Certificate Program, Dade Community College, 1992
Master's in Social Work, Columbia University, 1977
B.A., English, Hunter College, 1974

Interests

Deep-sea fishing, underwater photography, bridge

Resume of a Job Candidate Reentering the Work Force

Tamara is hoping to get back into a creative services position at a magazine after a hiatus of five years. During the time she was not working as an employee, she started her own successful at-home graphic design business while parenting her young child. Her challenge is to create a resume that will convey the strength of her creative skills relative to magazine sales promotion.

Weaknesses in the "Before" version:

- The word "Introducing" should be deleted
- The objective is too specific; it may preclude the candidate from being considered for other positions that interest her
- The typeface is too casual, even for a creative profession
- It's not necessary to indicate who you report to
- The words "responsible for" are not necessary
- Details about accomplishments are lacking
- There are no numbers to support or explain job responsibilities

Improvements in the "After" version:

- Typeface (Eurostile) is a better choice; it's jazzy, but readable
- Broadening job objective increases job hunter's chances of getting called
- Additional information under summary of qualifications fills out her profile
- Addition of accomplishments strengthens credentials
- Inclusion of numbers helps portray candidate's understanding of business
- Choice of functional areas support job objective
- Adding interests section with good detail provides insight into the person

Before

Introducing

Tamara Durell

624 Jamestown Lane
Blauvelt, New York 10450
914-555-6788
E•mail: TamaraD@aol.com

Job objective: Creative director at a women's magazine

Summary: Twenty years of experience as a graphic designer; ten years of promotion experience in magazines

Experience:

1990–1996
Principal, Tamara Durell Design
Worked part-time in my own home-based business.
Handled projects for an average of ten clients annually.
Worked on retainer for *Suburban Families*.
Did pro bono promotional work for The Bridge Preschool.

1985–1990
Creative Director, *East Coast Woman*, New York, NY
Helped reposition magazine with advertisers.
Administered a $1M budget.
Reported to publisher.
Responsible for development and direction of a full-service creative department.
Principal skills of creative direction are applied while working closely with sales management, editors, company management, and outside suppliers.
Handle creation of audiovisual presentations, trade advertising, sales development programs, convention and trade show participation, sales tools, and collateral.

1980–1985
Senior Art Director, Jensen, Boyle & Kone Advertising, New York, NY
Worked on accounts including Coty, Estee Lauder, and Samsonite.
Reported to vice president.
Responsible for a variety of design programs, including advertising campaigns, packaging, point-of-purchase displays, press kits, and exhibit designs.

1976–1980
Graphic Designer, Bay Area Regional Transit, San Francisco, CA
Designed pictograms and assisted in the development of signage systems for stations systemwide.
Responsible for design, construction and budget of area identification interior directional systems, and directories.
Reported to divisional manager.

Education: 1976, B.A., San Francisco State University

After

Tamara Durell

624 Jamestown Lane
Blauvelt, New York 10450
914-555-6788
E-mail: TamaraD@aol.com

Job Objective
Creative position in magazine sales promotion and marketing

Summary of Qualifications
Twenty years of experience as a graphic designer; ten years of promotion experience in magazines; five years of experience running my own business; staff supervisory skills; budget planning and management; sales support through innovative promotion tools

Areas of Expertise

SALES PROMOTION
- Developed comprehensive plan to launch magazine start-up, *Suburban Families*; created media kit and promotion materials; honored by publisher at second annual sales meeting for "playing an instrumental role in generating ad pages above expectations," 1996
- Helped reposition *East Coast Woman*, an eight-state publication; worked with outside advertising agency to develop new ad campaign aimed at advertisers, and directed efforts of five-person staff to create an audiovisual presentation for advertisers; ad pages increased 20 percent during my tenure, 1985–1990

MANAGEMENT
- Launched my own graphic design business from my home-based office after the birth of my first child; grossed average of $100K per year, 1990–1996
- Managed $1M promotion budget annually, 1985–1990
- Developed and directed five-person creative services department

GRAPHIC DESIGN
- Created first promotional brochure for The Bridge Preschool, which resulted in a 100 percent increase in applications to the school, 1995–96
- Devised and directed the creation of audiovisual presentations, trade advertising, sales development programs, convention and trade show participation, sales tools and collateral; have won ten design awards, 1985–1990
- Created advertising campaigns, packaging, point-of-purchase displays, press kits, and exhibit designs; accounts I worked on (Coty, Estee Lauder, Samsonite) nominated five times for awards, 1980–1990
- Designed pictograms and assisted in the development of signs systems for stations systemwide, 1976–1980

Work Experience
1990–1996	Principal, Tamara Durell Design
1985–1990	Creative Director, *East Coast Woman*, New York, NY
1980–1985	Senior Art Director, Jensen, Boyle & Kone Advertising, New York, NY
1976–1980	Graphic Designer, Bay Area Regional Transit, San Francisco, CA
Education	1976, B.A., San Francisco State University
Interests	Collecting Americana, competing in triathlons (have completed five), doing art therapy with children (have volunteered 100 hours annually for last five years)

THE COMBINATION CHRONOLOGICAL/ FUNCTIONAL FORMAT

The final two sets of resumes presented here use a combination chronological/ functional format. In addition to presenting your experience in an easy-to-read manner, it allows you to highlight the functional skills you have gained as a result of that experience.

Resume of a Recent Graduate

Eliza has worked for a manufacturer and a retailer part-time and during summers. Now that she has an associate degree in fashion merchandising, she'd like to make the leap to clothing buyer.

Weaknesses in the "Before" version:

- Using same size typeface and same indentation gives resume a bland look
- Putting all ID information on one line may result in misinformation if it's scanned
- Job accomplishments and responsibilities are not well analyzed
- Lack of number and details makes responsibilities sound ordinary
- Simple listing of job tasks doesn't promote candidate's potential to perform functions of a buyer

Improvements in the "After" version:

- Typeface (Optima) is clean and easy to read
- Each piece of ID information on its own line
- Use of caps, different indents, and type size creates more visually pleasing resume
- Identification of areas of expertise to relevant job tasks supports job objective
- Numbers and details strengthen candidate's experience
- Added explanation of interests a good idea

Before

Eliza Wong
700 N. Altmont Way, Montclair, NJ 09087   (201) 555-7890

Education: A.A., 1996, Fashion Merchandising, Bergen County Community College, 1994 graduate, Livingston High School

Work Experience:

Floater, Ellen Tracy Warehouse, Moonachie, NJ, Summers, 1994-95

- oversaw shipments of clothing to adjunct warehouse, including quality-control inspections and storage
- assisted in supervision of inspectors
- made decisions on which clothing flaws warranted garment being sent to factory store

Floor Assistant, Bloomingdales, Hackensack, NJ, Summers, 1992-93

- monitored flow of sales clerks to insure all stations covered
- helped designers to come up with department themes and seasonal displays
- made recommendations to buyers based on observations of inventory and customer buying habits

Sales Clerk, Bloomingdales, Hackensack, NJ, 1992-93 part-time

- developed experience in women's, children's, and men's fashion areas
- responsible for accurate financial transactions with customers

Interests: Sewing, hiking, singing

After

Eliza Wong
700 N. Altmont Way
Montclair, New Jersey 09087
201-555-7890

Objective
A position as a clothing or accessories buyer.

Education
A.A., 1996, Fashion Merchandising, Bergen County Community College

1994 graduate, Livingston High School

Work Experience

Floater, Ellen Tracy Warehouse, Moonachie, NJ, Summers, 1994-95

SUPERVISION Oversaw shipments of clothing worth up to $50,000 to adjunct warehouse,
Assisted in supervision of inspectors

QUALITY CONTROL Decided which clothing flaws warranted garment being sent to factory store

Conducted inspections of clothing for flaws and damage

Floor Assistant, Bloomingdales, Hackensack, NJ, Summers, 1992–93

SUPERVISION Monitored flow of sales clerks to insure all stations covered

MERCHANDISING Worked with designers to come up with department themes and seasonal displays

Made recommendations to buyers based on observations of inventory and customer buying habits

Sales Clerk, Bloomingdales, Hackensack, NJ, 1992–93, part-time

MERCHANDISING Developed sense of consumer buying habits and preferences by talking with customers in women's, children's, and men's fashion areas

SALES Got involved in customer decision making by helping to accessorize and style look

Interests
Sewing (have created my own designs and sold over 100 items), hiking in the Adirondacks, singing in local choir

Resume of a Job Candidate Changing Careers

Sheryl Jamison has been a writer and editor for sixteen years and has occasionally taught writing courses. She now wants to change careers and move into a full-time faculty position at a university.

Weaknesses in the "Before" version:

- Typeface unusual
- Curriculum vitae often used on resumes in academia, but not necessary
- ID elements appear on same line; could result in misinformation if scanned
- No variation in type size, use of caps
- Lacks job objective, which would be helpful
- No analysis of how experience would help her function well as a professor

Improvements in the "After" version

- Clean, easy-to-read typeface (Palatino)
- Variation in type size provides visual interest and easy identification of categories
- Addition of job objective helpful
- Good analysis of functional skills needed for teaching; excellent support points provided
- Editing of otherwise strong work experience section eliminates repetition
- Positioning of teaching experience first a good idea
- Creation of awards section a good idea

Before

Curriculum Vitae
Sheryl Jamison

26 West 75th Street
New York, NY 10023

(212) 555-9823 (h)
(212) 555-9000 (w)

Experience

Crain's New York Business 1990-present

Senior editor, 1993-present

- Generate, assign, and edit one third of this business weekly
- Write occasional full-length features, particularly profile pieces
- Oversee work off contributing editors and freelance staff
- Coordinate editorial with design staff and serve as a liaison with production and research departments

Editor, Media Department, 1990-1993

- Covered the media beat and wrote more than fifty news stories and features
- Covered the real estate beat and wrote more than thirty-five news stories, features, and a weekly real estate wrap-up
- Interviewed top business people, including magazine publishers and editors, book publishers and editors, owners of media companies, and Wall Street media analysts

Business Week, 1980-1990

Staff editor, 1985-1990

- Reported and edited stories with an emphasis on major economic trends, corporate marketing strategies, and advertising news.
- Originated story ideas and worked closely with domestic and international bureaus.

Reporter, 1980-1985

- Developed story ideas for company profiles and trend stories; wrote fifteen cover stories and ten major inside features
- Won Overseas Press Club young reporter award for series on impact of American companies relocating manufacturing plants abroad

Teaching

New York University School of Journalism
Adjunct Professor, 1992-present

- Teach news and feature writing courses to undergraduates (one per year); earned "10" rating in student evaluations, the highest rating possible

Education

M.A., Columbia School of Journalism, 1980
B.A., Pennsylvania State University, 1979

Interests

Karate, folk guitar, crossword puzzles

After

Sheryl Jamison

26 West 75th Street
New York, NY 10023(212)
555-9000 (w)
E-mail: 77777.5555 (CompuServe)

Job Objective A full-time faculty position within the journalism department of a university

Areas of Expertise

TEACHING

- Taught news and feature writing courses to undergraduates
- Earned "10" rating in student evaluations, the highest possible rating
- Developed and moderated two of ten special panels for journalism faculty and students during the 1995–96 years

EDITING AND WRITING

- Developed story ideas, conducted research, wrote story proposals
- Interviewed business leaders, Wall Street analysts, economists, company presidents, and government officials
- Have written more than 200 business trend stories, profiles, and features

COMMUNICATION

- Edited stories of top business writers and columnists, with whom I developed friendly and productive working relationships
- Volunteered to work as journalism department ombudsman to resolve student-faculty disagreements
- Coordinated editorial with design staff and served as a liaison with production and research departments

New York University School of Journalism
Adjunct Professor, 1992–present

- Teach news and feature writing courses to undergraduates (one per year)

Crain's New York Business, **1990–present**
Senior editor, 1993–present

- Generate, assign, and edit one third of this business weekly
- Oversee work off contributing editors and freelance staff

Editor, Media Department, 1990–1993

- Covered the media beat and wrote more than fifty news stories and features
- Covered the real estate beat and wrote more than thirty-five news stories, features, and a weekly real estate wrap-up

---

Business Week, **1980–1990**
Staff editor, 1985–1990

- Reported and edited stories with an emphasis on major economic trends, corporate marketing strategies, and advertising news
- Originated story ideas and worked closely with domestic and international bureaus

Reporter, 1980–1985

- Developed story ideas for company profiles and trend stories; wrote fifteen cover stories and ten major inside features

Awards   Won Overseas Press Club young reporter award for series on impact of American companies relocating manufacturing plants abroad

Education   M.A., Columbia School of Journalism, 1980
B.A., Pennsylvania State University, 1979

Interests   Karate (brown belt); playing folk guitar; doing crossword puzzles

Conduct a Winning Job Search with These New Peterson's Titles

e 90-Minute Interview Prep Book

gy Schmidt

e perfect companion to *The 90-Minute Resume*, it shows
how to make preparing for job interviews easy and
ective by working with a "coach"—friend, spouse, colleague,
even yourself. *Free software* provides checklists and
luation forms for critiquing your presentation style.
N 634-0, 160 pp., 8 1/2 x 11, **$15.95 pb**

e Job Hunter's Word Finder

nes Bluemond

e your resume or cover letter the needed extra "punch"
h an A-Z guide to thousands of synonyms for overused
rds, the latest industry-specific buzzwords for 100 career
ds, and key words for each job position.
N 600-6, 224 pp., 6 x 9, **$11.95 pb**

rsonal Job Power

y Carr and Valorie Beer

lps you survive—and thrive—in today's uncertain business
rld. Shows you how to develop and use personal power
ectively. Identifies seven different "power types" and
ows how each one works.
N 599-9, 224 pp., 6 x 9, **$12.95 pb**

dden Job Market 1997

vides you with detailed contact information on the nation's
00 fastest-growing small to mid-size companies—those that
hiring at four times the national rate! Covers a wide range
high-growth industries such as environmental consulting,
etic engineering, and computers.
N 644-8, 320 pp., 6 x 9, **$18.95 pb**

b Opportunities in Business 1997

scribes 2,000 of the leading fastest-growing U.S. companies in
service and trade sectors as well as manufacturing and
ustrial firms.
N 646-4, 334 pp., 8 1/2 x 11, **$21.95 pb**

b Opportunities in Engineering Technology 1997

files some 2,000 companies at the leading edge of high-
hnology in areas such as biotechnology, telecommunications,
ware, computers and peripherals, and consumer electronics.
N 647-2, 432 pp., 8 1/2 x 11, **$21.95 pb**

b Opportunities in Health Care 1997

ntifies hiring organizations in the health-care field, including
dical equipment and supply companies, pharmaceutical firms,
lth insurance and managed-care companies, skilled nursing
e facilities, hospitals, and medical laboratories.
N 648-0, 220 pp., 8 1/2 x 11, **$21.95 pb**

N *Prefix: 1-56079-*

Available at Fine Bookstores Near You

Or Order Direct
Call: 800-338-3282
Fax: 609-243-9150

Visit Peterson's Education & Career Center
on the Internet
http://www.petersons.com

P Peterson's Princeton, NJ